Doodle Me This...

By Mary Dooley

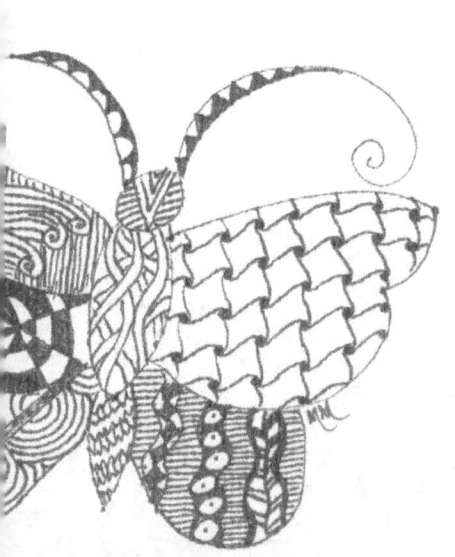

Adult Coloring and Doodling book

Doodle Me This...

For Lily and Emma

Oh, and you.

(Yes, you!)

Also by
Mary Dooley:

Espresso Yourself
- Bits of Wisdom from the Coffee Shop

Espresso Yourself TOO
- Wisdom From the Coffee Shop

Hello everyone!

If you THINK you're not an artist,
I am going to help you become one!

If you are an artist, I am going to give
you some new ideas!

Stay tuned. I promise it will be fun!

Enjoy,

Mary

P.S. From here on out, doodling, drawing and coloring are all part of the whole, when you see ◭ , all are meant.

P.P.S. Use white space all throughout the book for ◭ !

There are two kinds of artists in the world.

BOTH are very important.

1. The artist who likes everything perfect.

You like perfect lines, perfect colors and perfect outcomes.

In art those things are important!

Use your strengths!

HOWEVER you can, in no way, make perfect art.

Know THAT at the outset, and your joy will increase...

Reframe your thinking and get perfectly crooked once in a while.

2. The artist who likes everything not so perfect.

You like the waves, curves and angles.

In art those things are important!

Use your strengths!

HOWEVER you can, in some way, make a not so perfect straight line.

Know THAT at the outset, and your joy will increase...

Reframe your thinking and get imperfectly straight once in a while.

Practice your first doodle here!

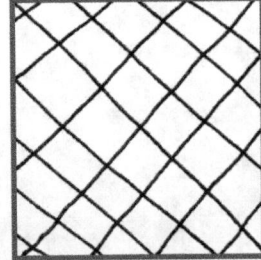 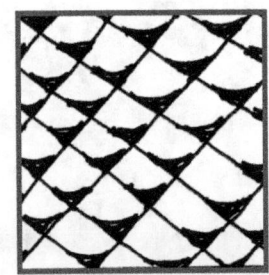 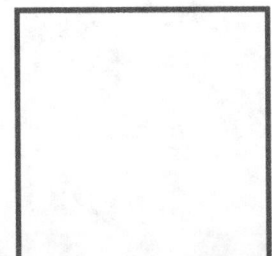 

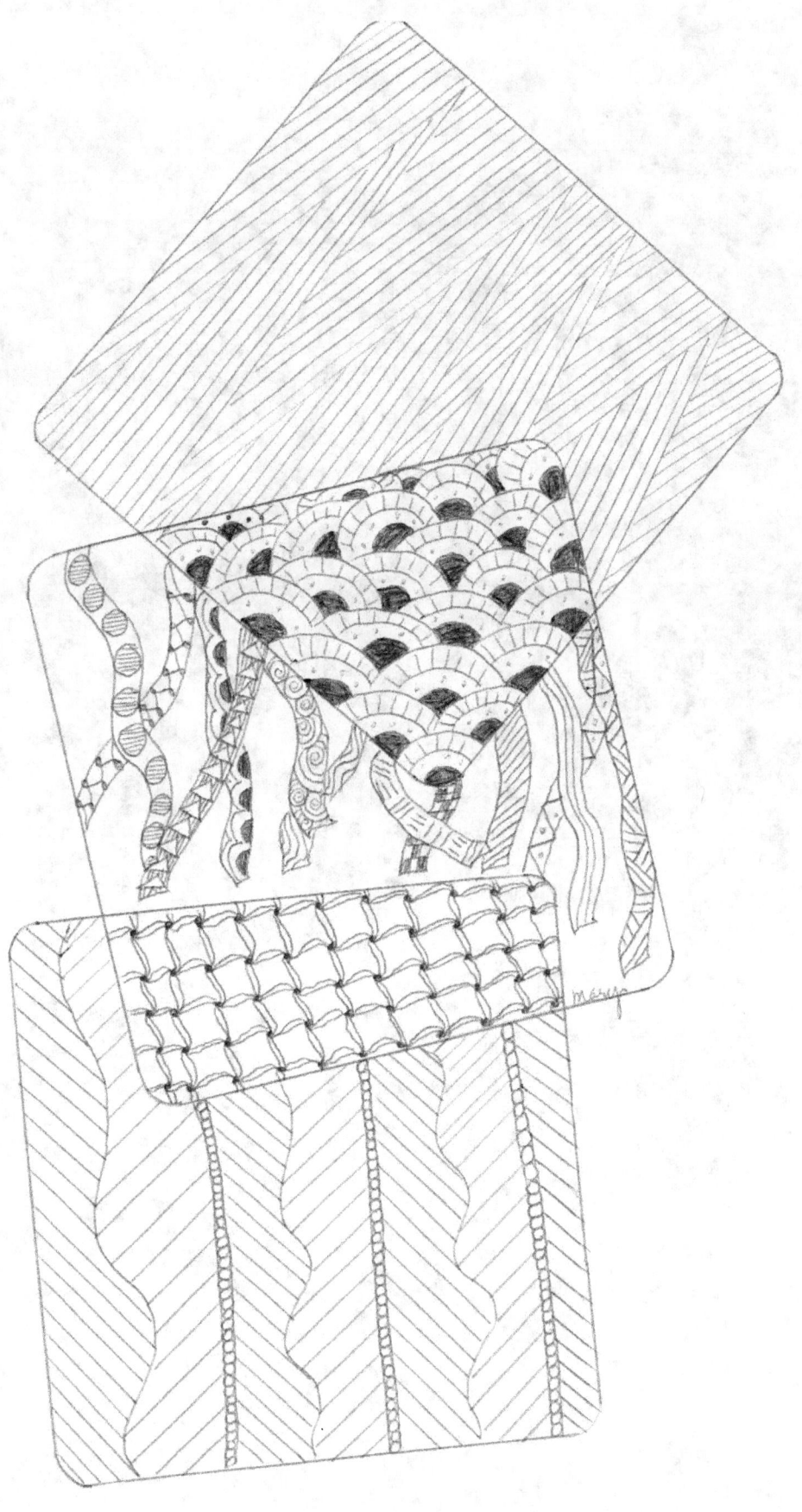

Soweto, thank you for your mad, mad, mad wild skills

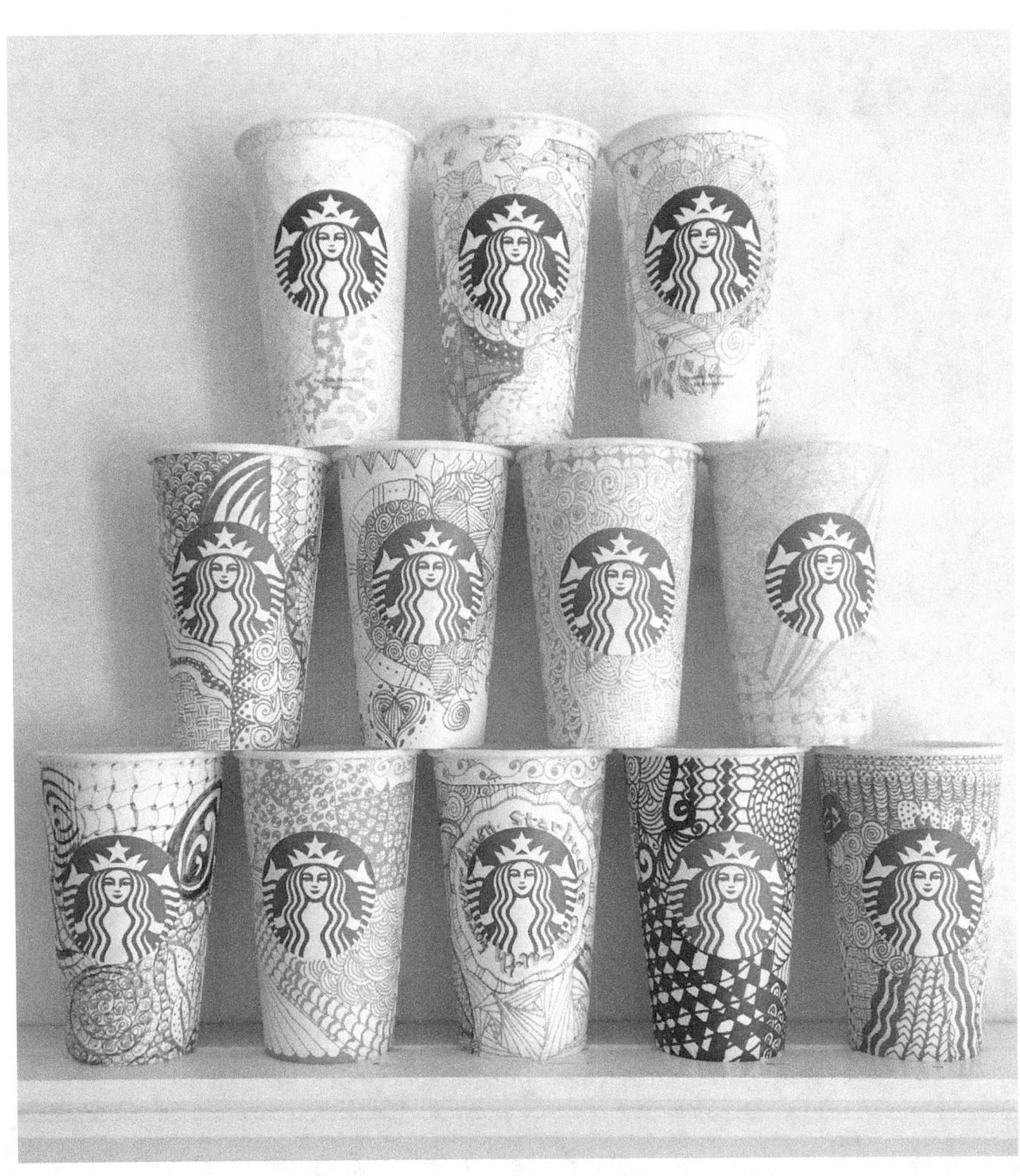

Doodle Me This

Blame it on the CUPS!

About six years ago I started to get serious about my doodling.

Can you believe I used serious AND doodling in the same sentence?

It's true.

I started working for Starbucks and I stumbled across these crazy amazing

cup doodlings/drawings online.

I became obsessed.

These cups looked so cool! I wanted to be able to create them.

I set about learning how.. MANY, MANY, MANY hours of drawing

and MANY, MANY, MANY cups later.

Here are my creations...

⇦ ⇦ ⇦ ⇦ ⇦ ⇦

This lead to 🍕 all the time. Why?

Because along the way I also learned that while doodling:

* I could relax and focus on the moment.

* I could calm and rest my soul. (much needed for me)

* my conscious mind could become more creative and

inspired the more time I spent drawing.

* my unconscious mind could work on other goings-on in my life.

* 🍕 was bringing me joy!

How to enjoy this book.

Let the browsing begin.

Sure, look through the book first.

Get an idea of what YOU are going to create!

It does not matter where you begin.

Start.

No rules.

Grab any pen/pencil/crayon and go try something.
ANYWHERE.

Go now.

Color one small section. I am going to wait here.

Throughout your book there are boxes.

Each box shows a step by step example.

There are also blank boxes alongside for you to practice.

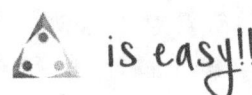 is easy!!

All art is made up of squiggles or circles or lines...

Draw a swirl...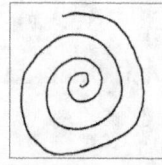

How about a square swirl...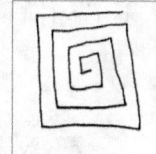

How about a triangle swirl...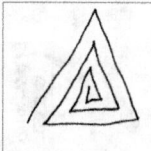

How about a circle inside a cirle...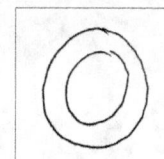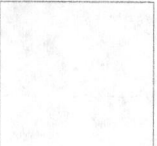

A square inside a square...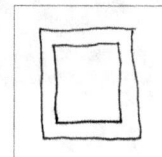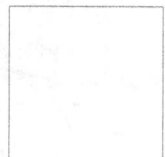

A square inside a circle inside a triangle...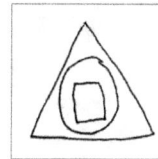

You are ⟁ing!

Let's ⟁ more and see what happens...

Favorite Tools

ANY old pen/pencil will do!

If you don't have any idea what to get, start with these!

If you like the way they work on the page - use them!

If not try something new.

Art supply stores have TONS of choices.

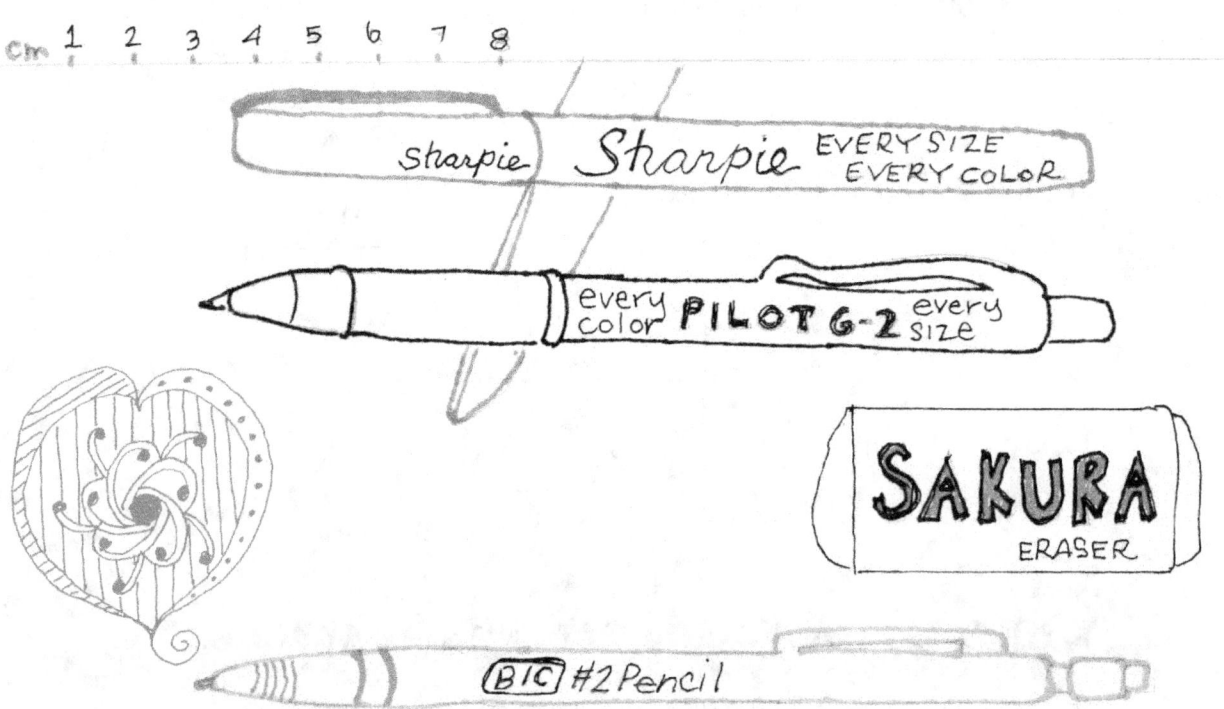

Try your tools.
Color, draw, scribble
doodle, and change
your tool.

Now pick a color
that makes you
happy, fill in the
circles.

Time to learn the ropes.

Take an 8.5 x 11 sheet of paper. (for practice just use copy paper.)

Fold the sheet in half. Then fold it again. Then cut along the folds.

You now have 4 boxes. Correct?

Take each box and draw a smaller box inside.

Now let's leave out the inside box -
NO
BOUNDARIES!

Patterns are drawn one step at a time.

Use these patterns to practice. Then use them in the boxes on previous page.

Separate those boxes into 2 sections and use both patterns in each box randomly.

Now do it a few more times using the patterns in a different way.

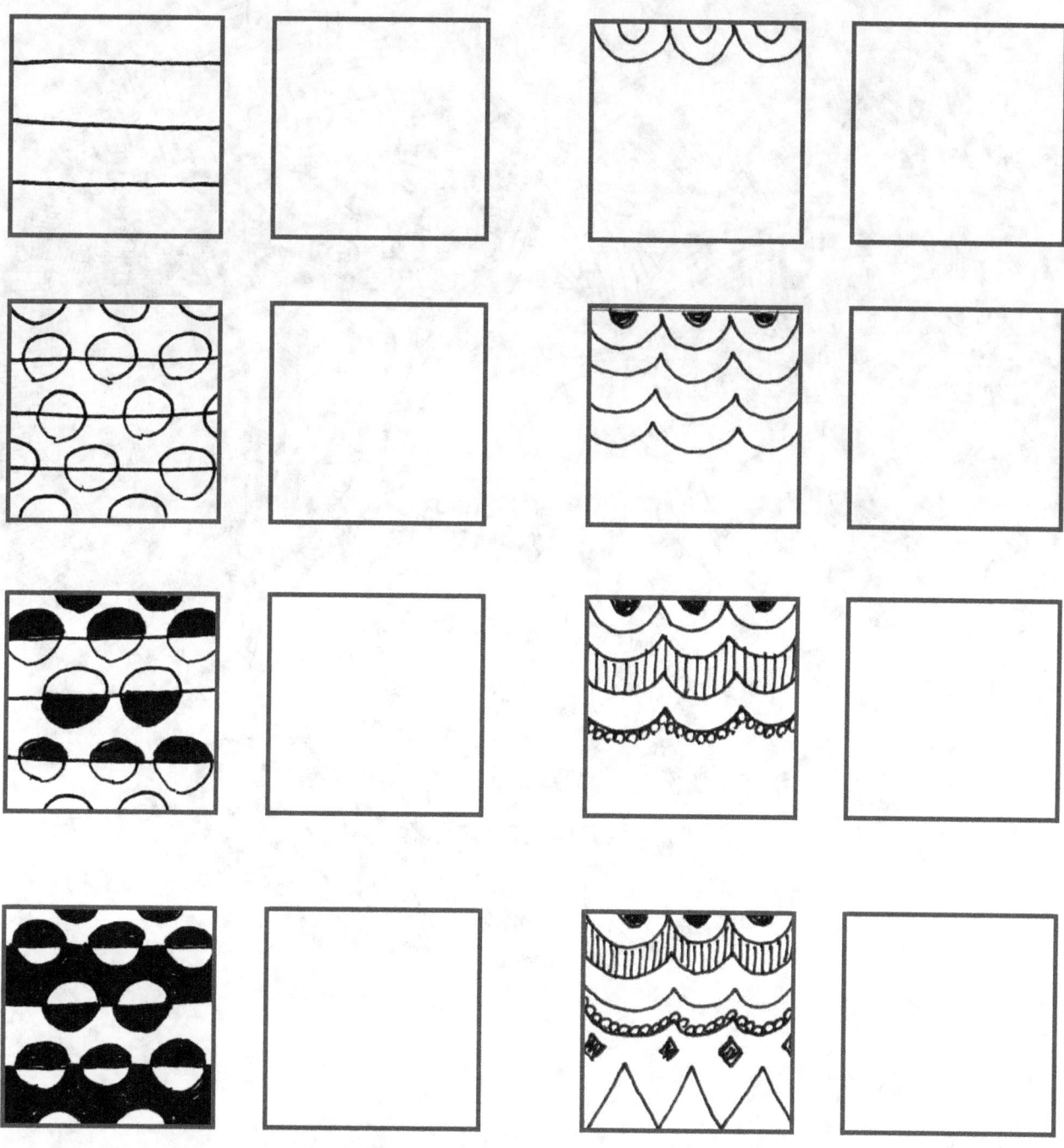

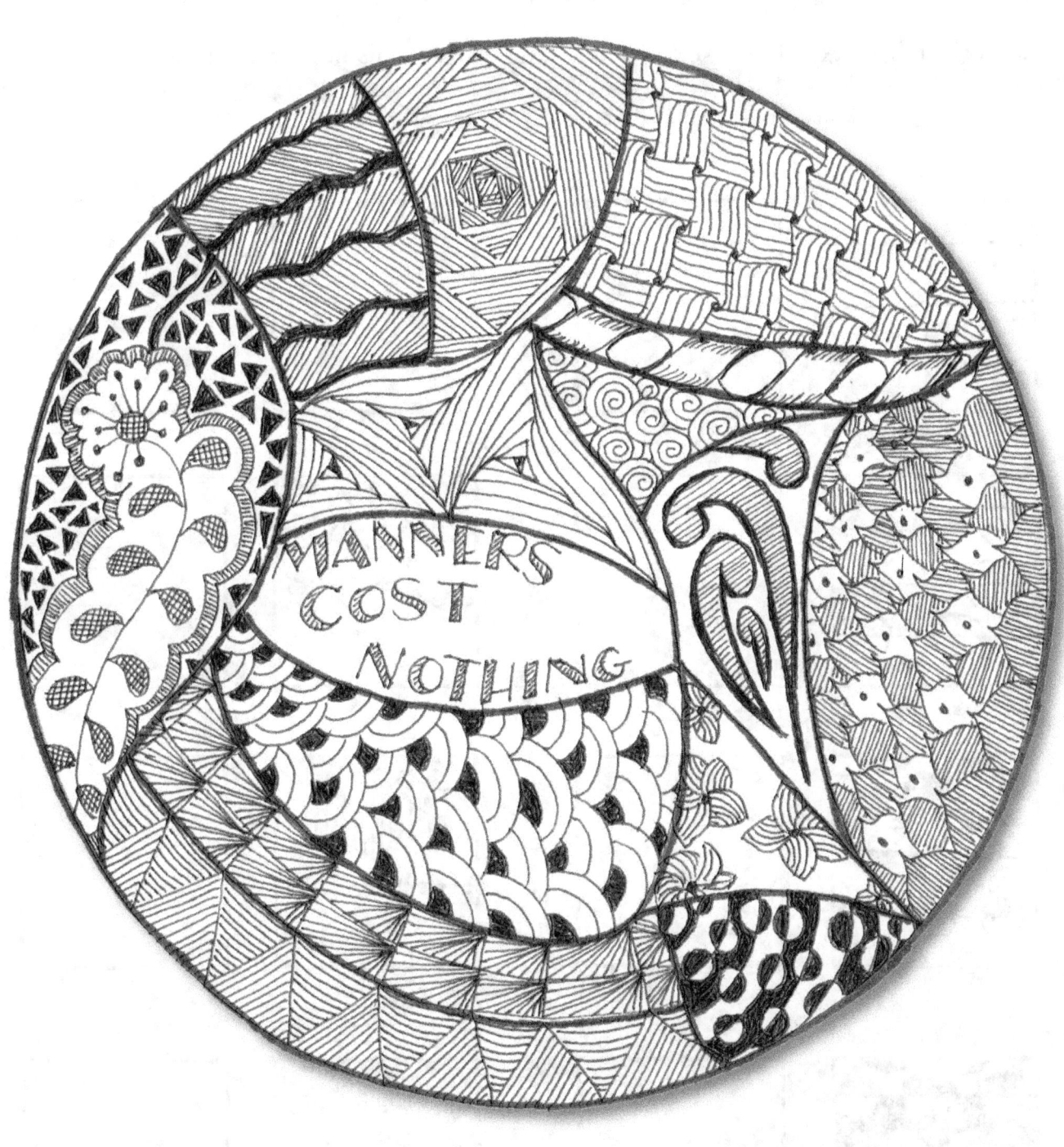

Doodle Me This

These patterns are in the picture on left. Can you find them?

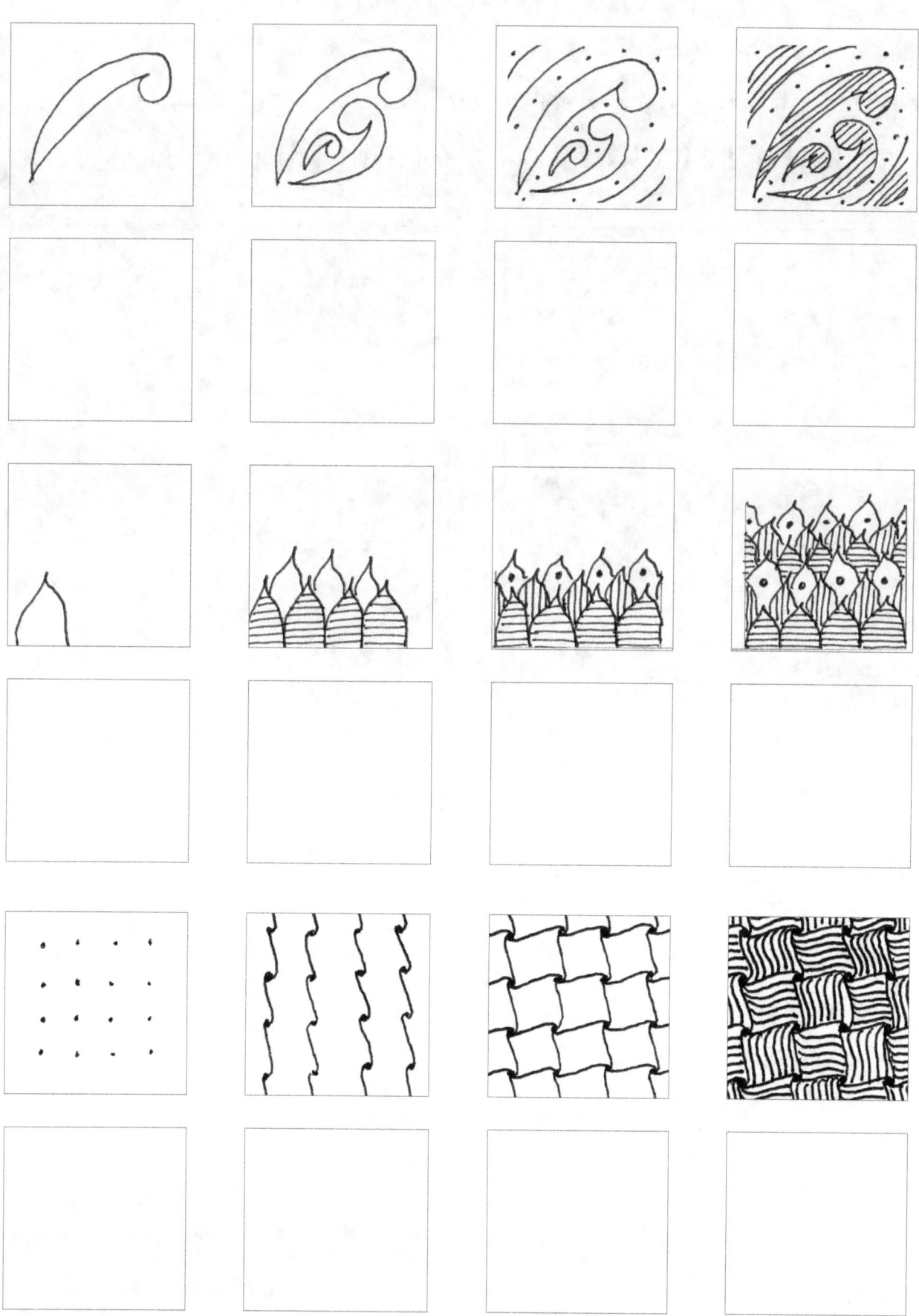

Mix and match.

Use patterns to create your own style in each box.

Section the areas INSIDE boxes then mix and match patterns!

Doodle Me This

Now use patterns OUTSIDE the areas...
Trial and error - that's how it works.

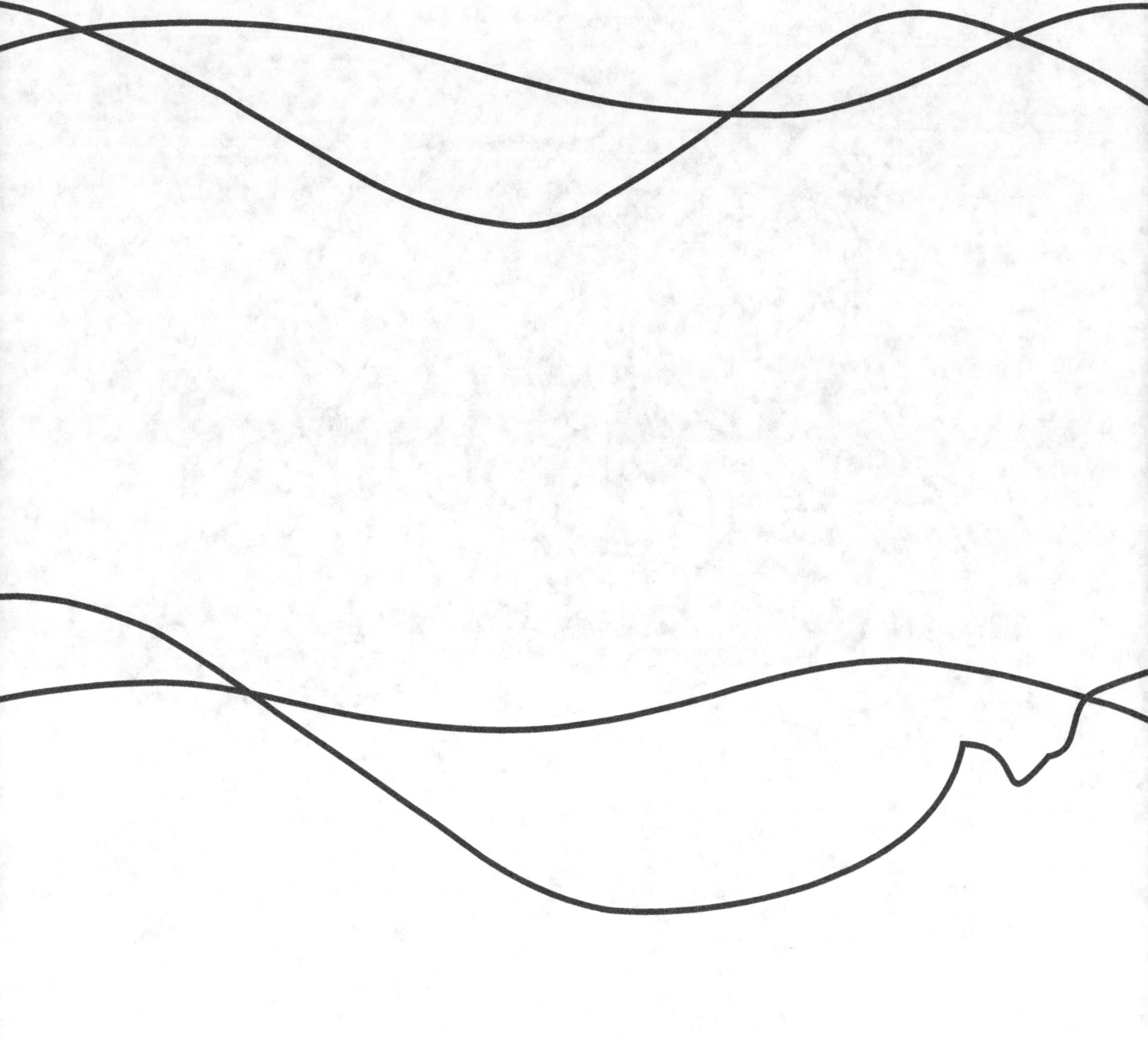

Most likely not perfect . but they are lovely!

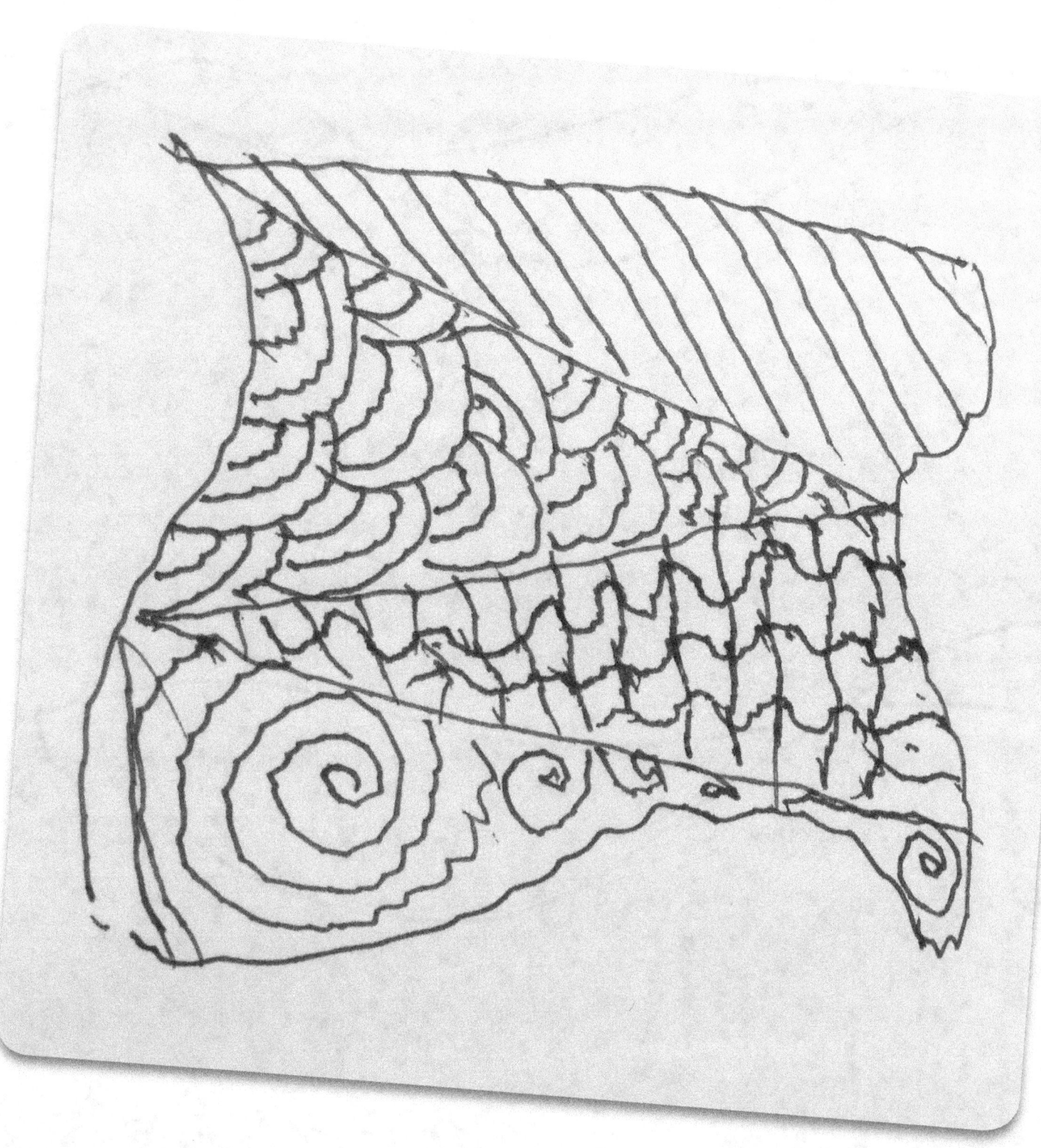

Doodle Me This

If you still think you can't 🔺, read this...

I teach art.

I always start with a story. If I can hook my students at the beginning, I will have their attention for the night. The goal is for everyone to relax and have fun. This is an easy-going class. I promise that EVERYONE who enters the classroom will exit an artist. Some laugh. That's okay I will laugh later!

Okay, keep that in the back of your mind, I'll circle back around to it.

Ten Minutes AFTER the start of one class, the door opens and in walks a very old man pushing a very old lady in a wheelchair. It takes a bit to get her situated. He says he will come back at the end of class. It's awkward. I do not like awkward. I greet the woman and get back into the groove of the lesson. It takes me a bit, However we move on.

I get into the witty repartee, which I am (in my own mind) famous for. I like to ask questions and I found out Claire was a retired hall/lunch lady in the local high school. She never had the chance to take any art classes. YES, yes I did apologize for any pain I may have caused any hall/lunch ladies during my school years.

Did I mention Claire is OLD?
AND she has arthritis,
AND shakes very badly
AND has a patch over one eye?

We are all clear she signed up for a drawing class, at night, RIGHT?

We begin drawing and I am still trying to figure out how to put her at ease. I hear her sigh and I say, "getting old is so stinkin' hard, isn' t it?" Immediately she relaxes, giggles and agrees. The others in the room start to relax also.

As I am walking around the room, I check on her and she is drawing!!
Arthritis, eye patch, shaking, and she is drawing!
Is her work perfect?
No.
Is it art? You betcha!
She kept drawing and I could tell the later it got, the harder she struggled.

But she kept drawing.

After class I usually like to cut and run. Tonight however, Claire wants to stay after and chat about an idea she has for using her doodling to create a large butterfly. Just then her husband comes in and looks at her, then at her work and tells me they have been married 67 years and he would do it all over again.
Why? Because now he can say he married an ARTIST.

Claire entered thinking she was, IN NO WAY, an artist.
She definitely exited an ARTIST.

IF CLAIRE CAN 🔺 , SO CAN YOU!

Wouldn't you agree?

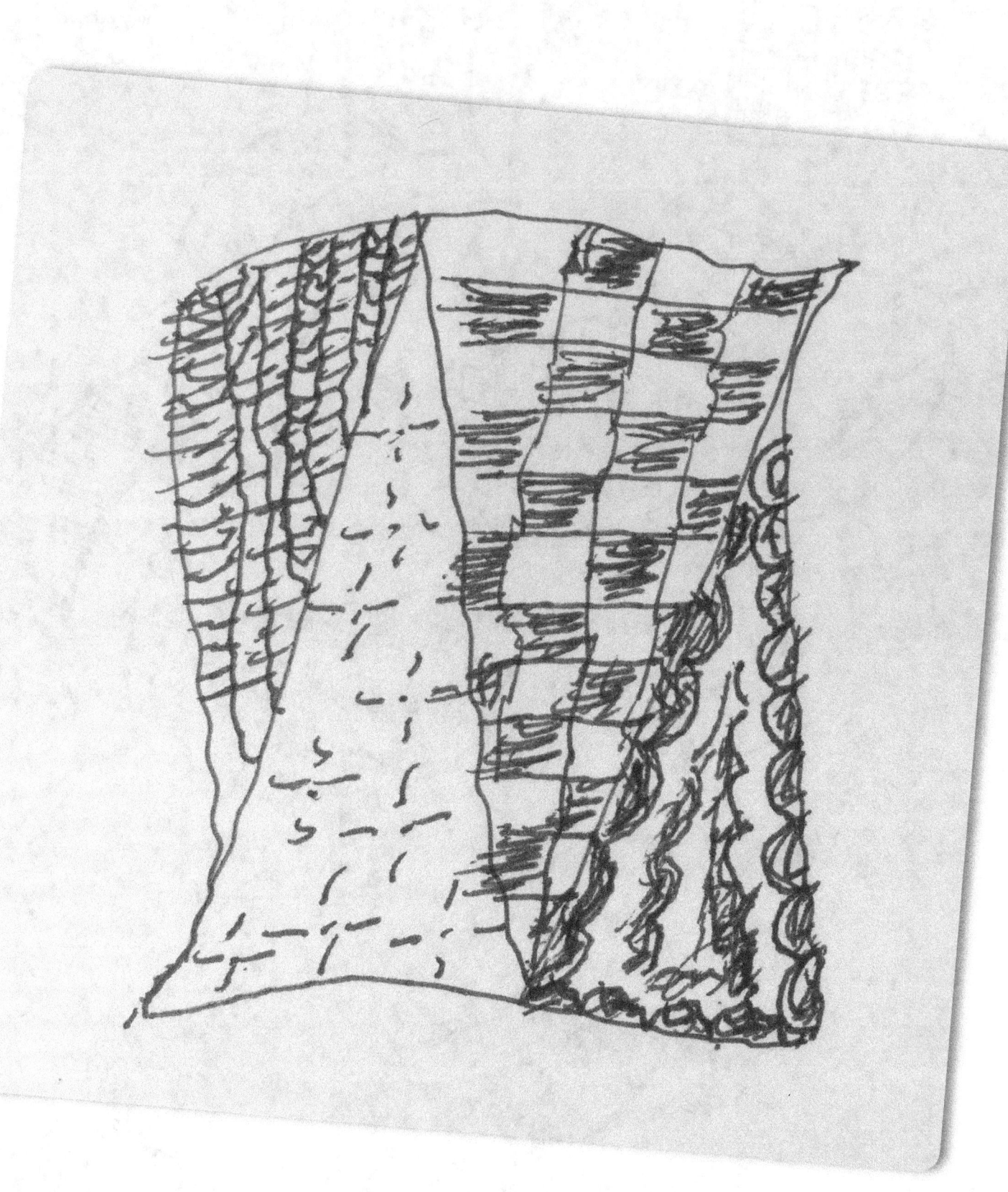

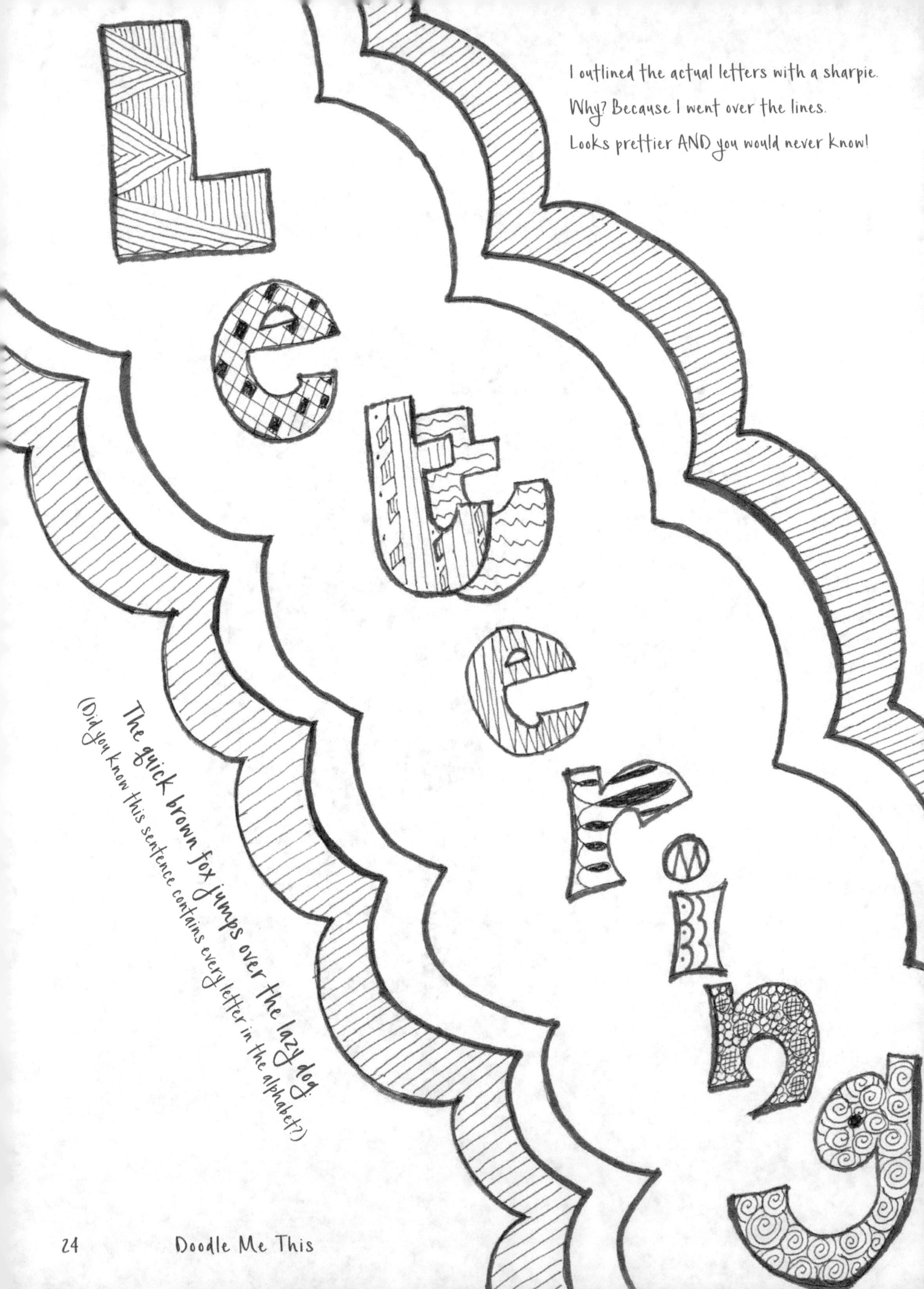

I outlined the actual letters with a sharpie.
Why? Because I went over the lines.
Looks prettier AND you would never know!

The quick brown fox jumps over the lazy dog.
(Did you know this sentence contains every letter in the alphabet?)

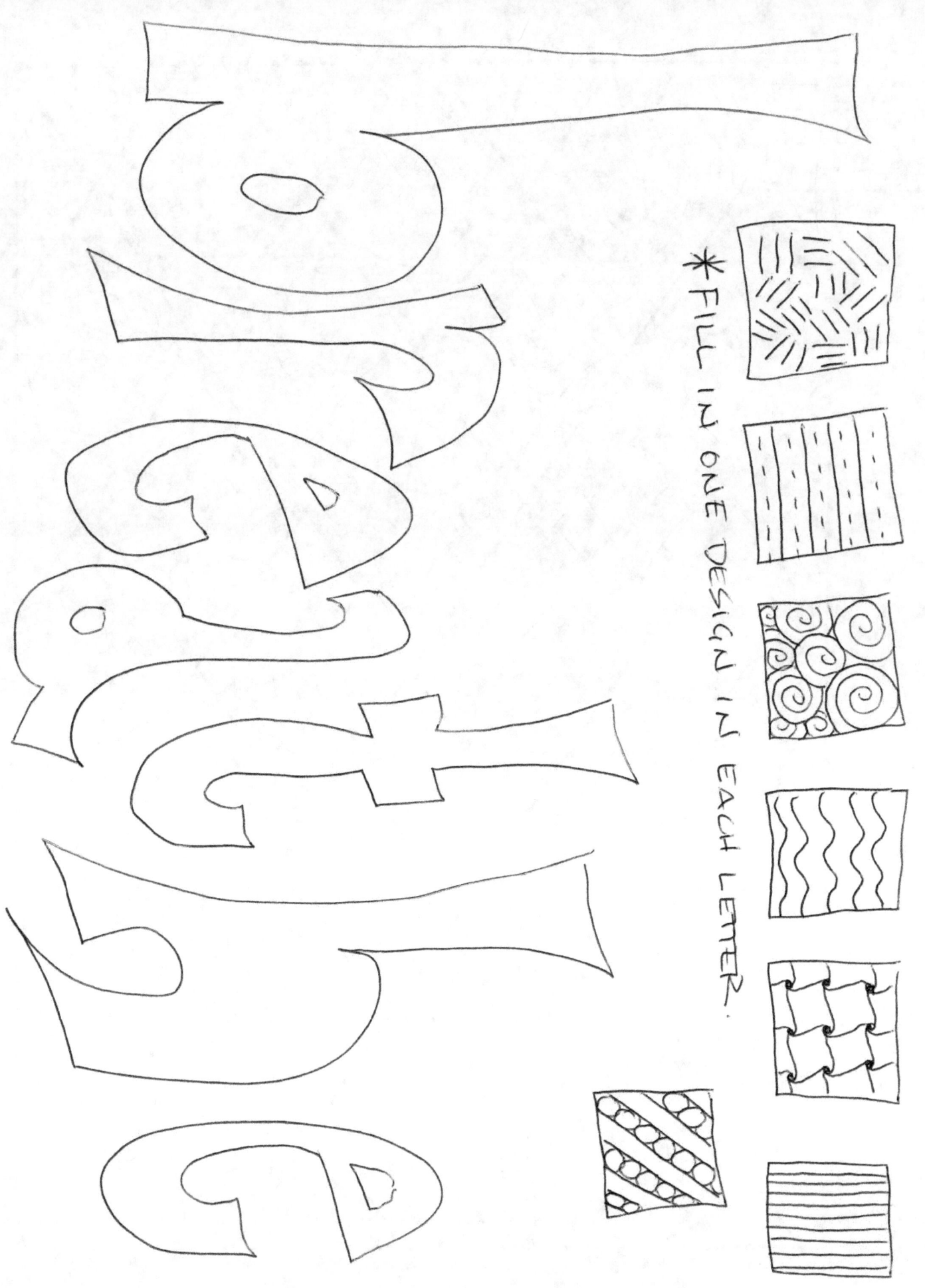

* FILL IN ONE DESIGN IN EACH LETTER.

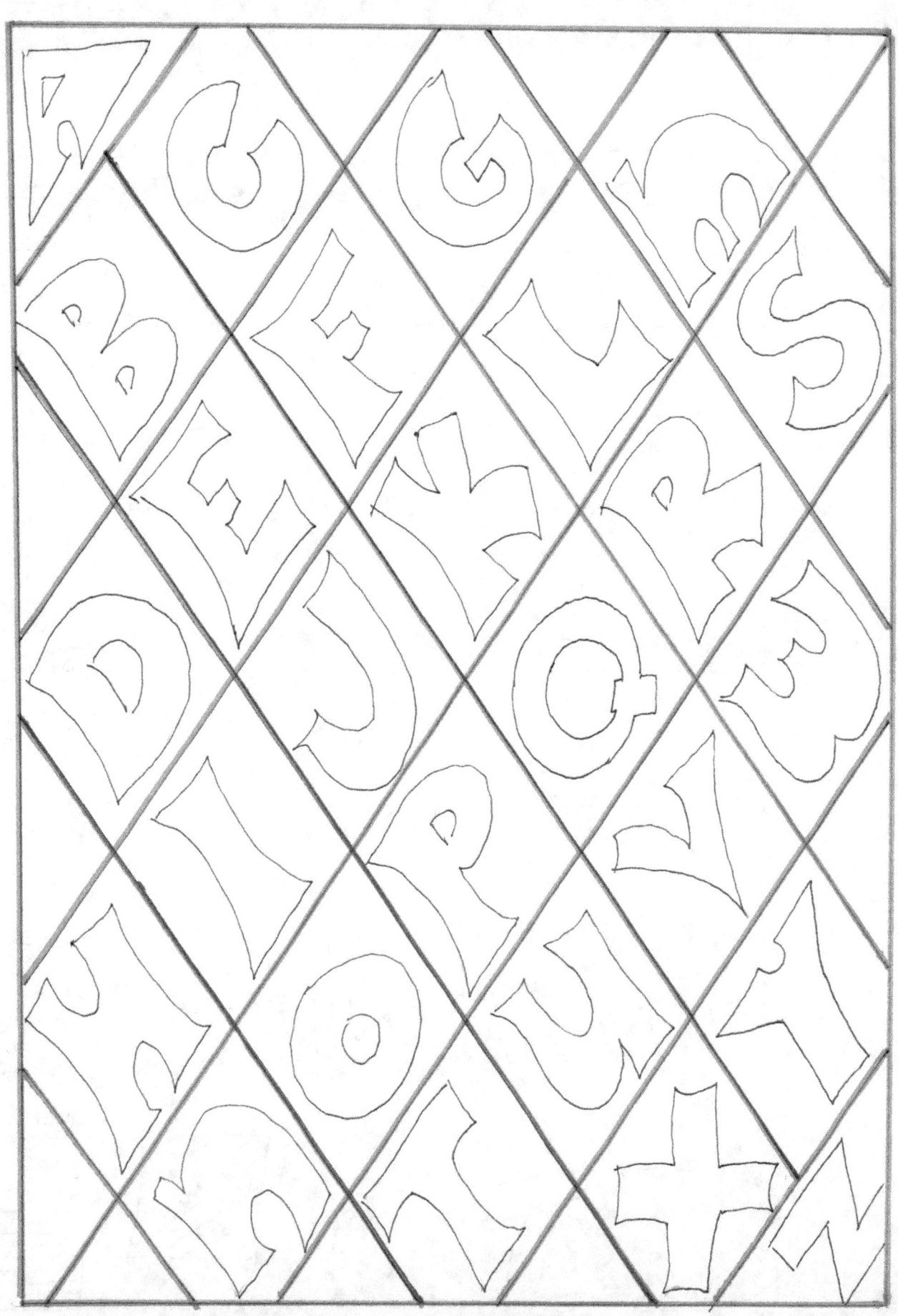

Doodle Me This

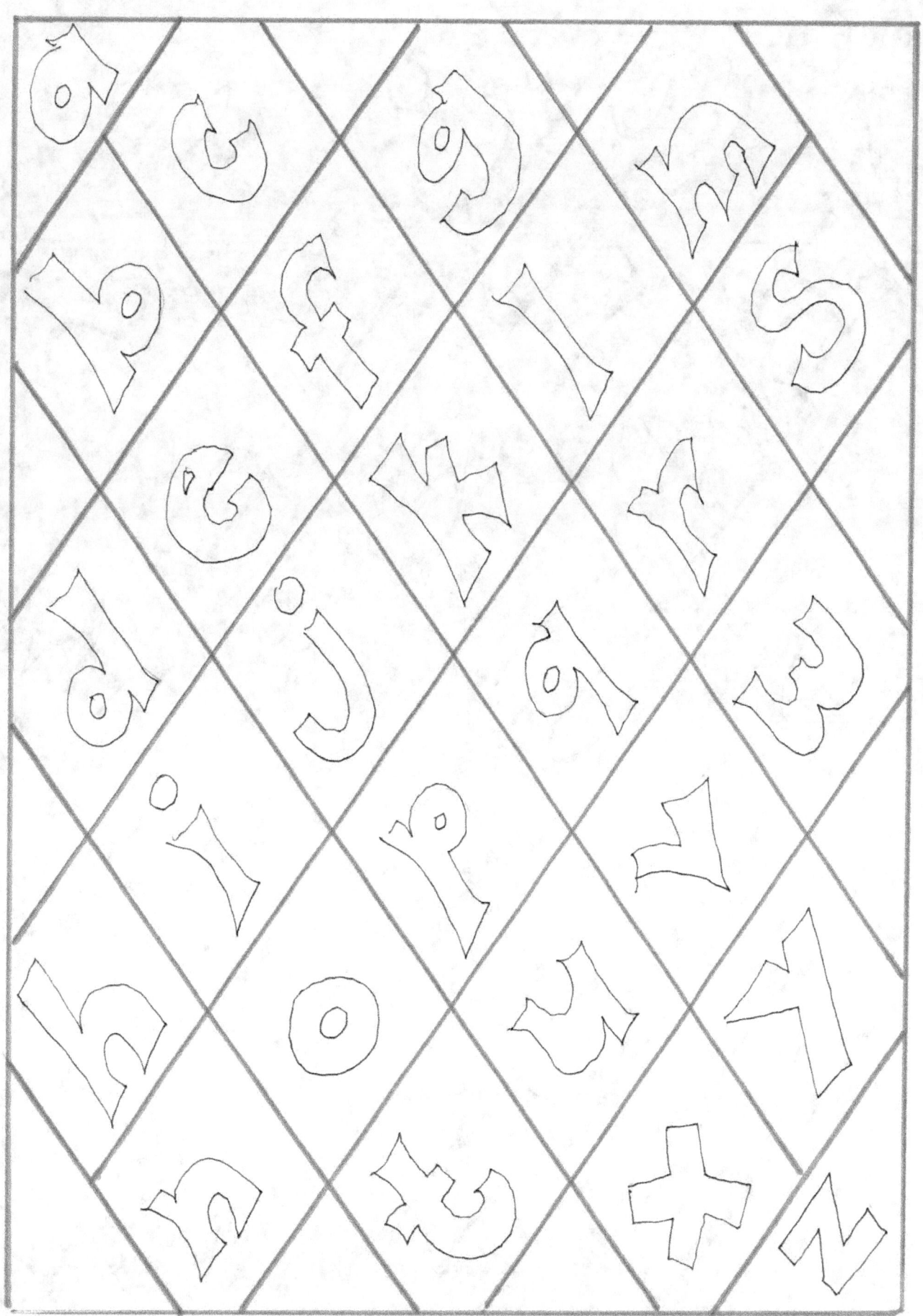

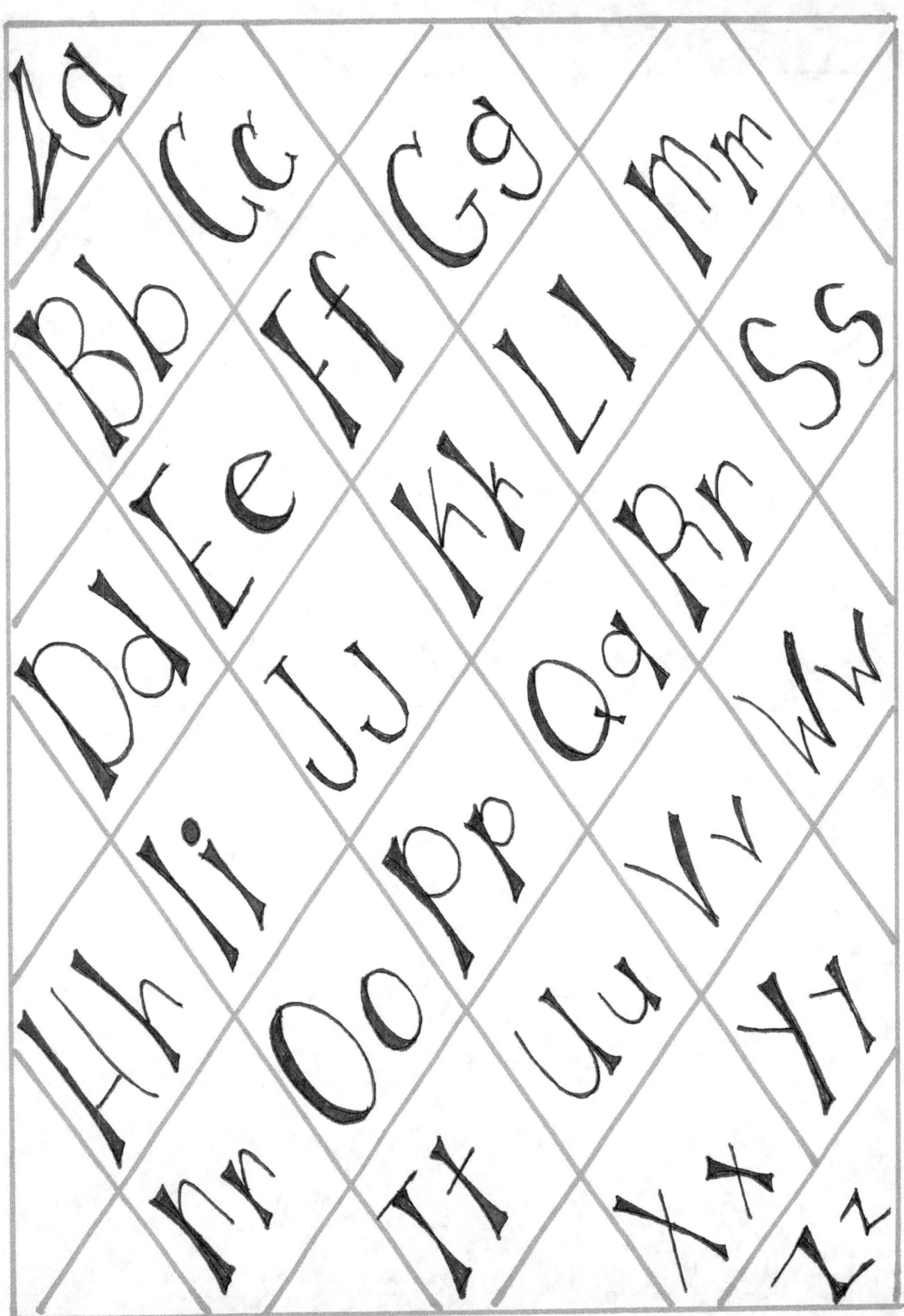

Doodle Me This

Using the alphabet...

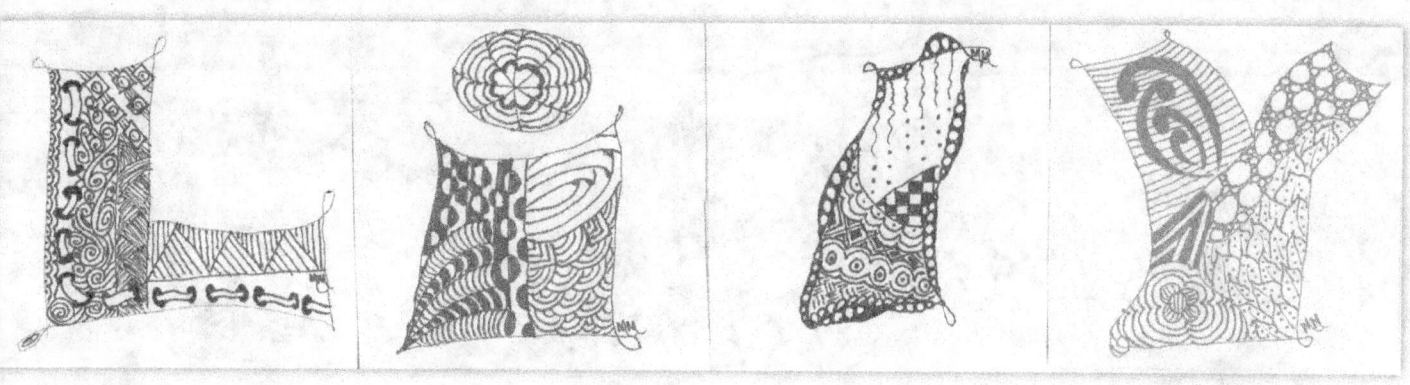

I created these letters on a piece of cardstock cut into four.

Taped together, not pretty but meaningful.

Cute, right?

Now create your own.

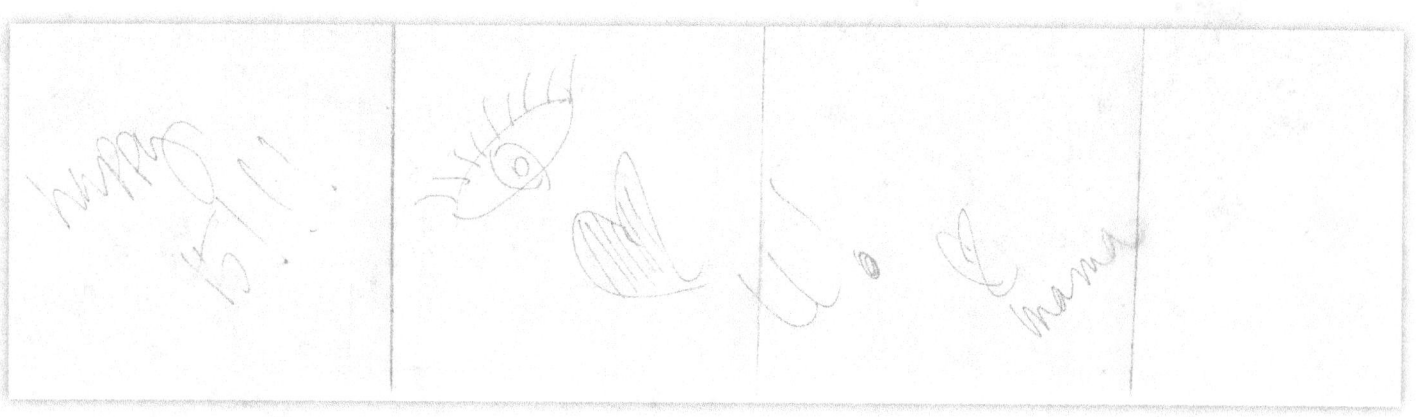

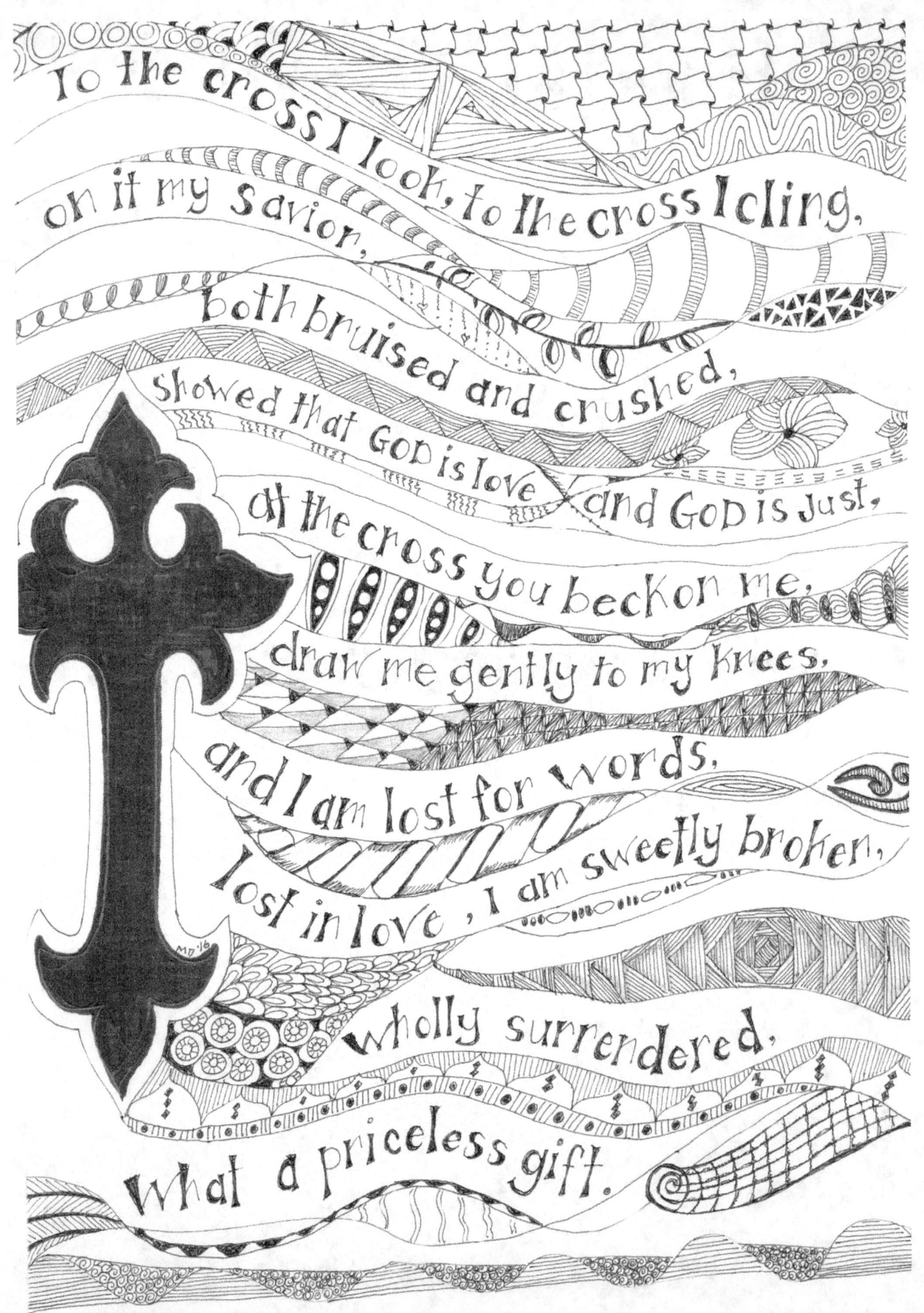

To the cross I look, to the cross I cling,
on it my savior,
both bruised and crushed,
showed that God is love and God is just,
at the cross you beckon me,
draw me gently to my knees,
and I am lost for words,
lost in love, I am sweetly broken,
wholly surrendered,
what a priceless gift.

Perfection

If you think this picture is perfect - look at this...

This is the process I took:

1. Drew lines in waves across the page in pencil.

2. Picked the lyrics I wanted.

3. Tried & failed (erased) many times!

4. Wrote a line or two of text and then a line or two of doodles.

5. Traced over with pen, eeeek!

6. It took a long time! I would walk away and start again later.

7. It never starts out pretty.

8. YOUR TURN!

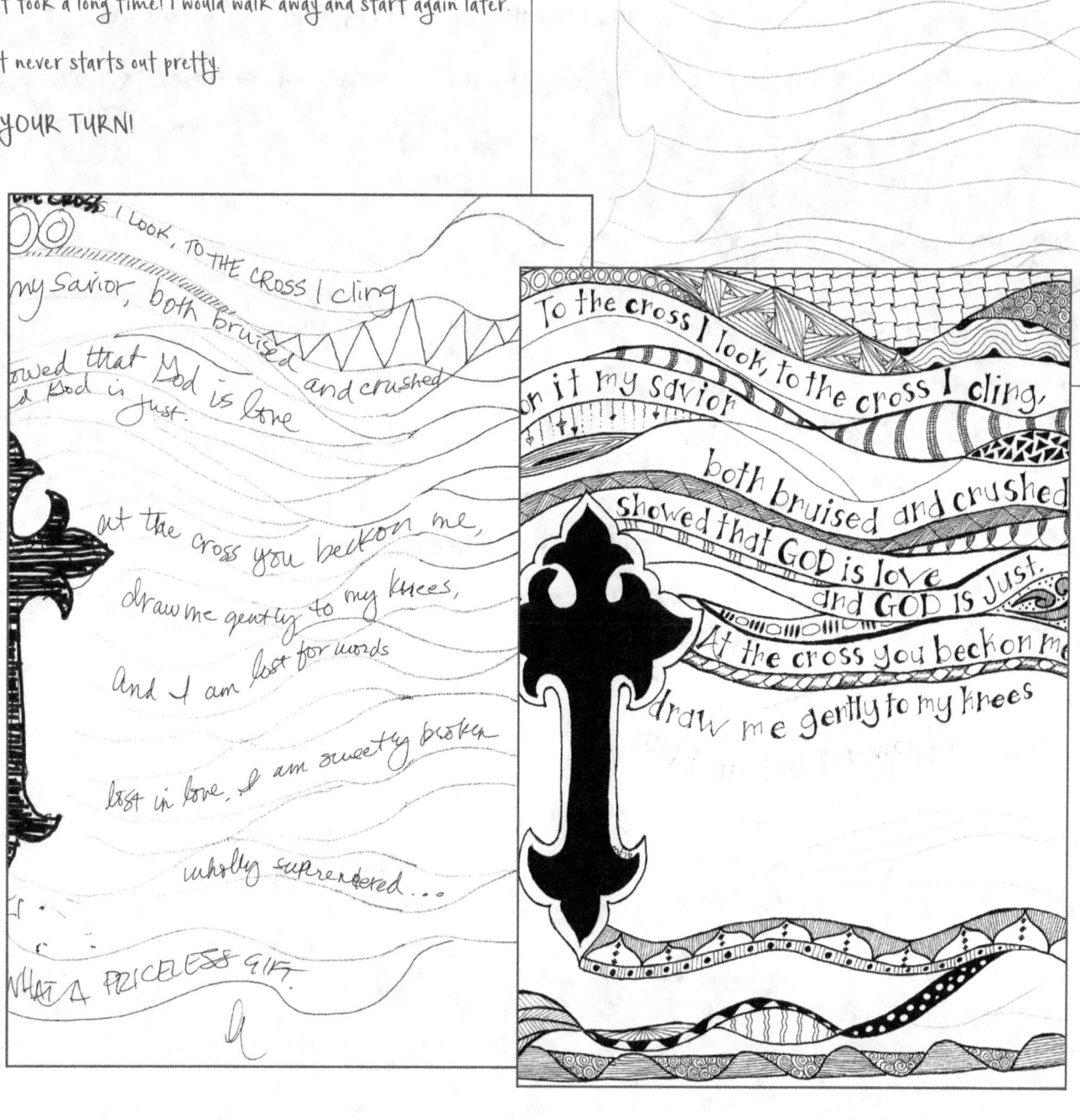

I am so glad you are still here.

At a recent fall celebration, I was coloring with sharpies on pumpkins. Well into a pretty good doodle of a jack-o-lantern, a little girl about four years old stopped by to look. I asked her if she wanted to try. She shook her head up and down and I handed her the sharpie. She started doodling all around what I had already drawn. Her mother walked up and was appalled, started apologizing, trying to take the sharpie away from her daughter. I told her it was okay. Yes, my drawing was pretty good, but we all need to start somewhere. Her mother couldn't stand it. Her daughter was "ruining" my pumpkin.

I disagree.

Given a choice, I would teach someone to 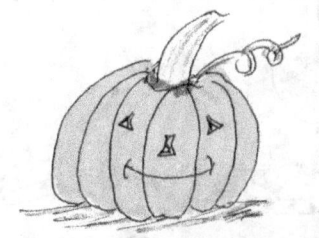 over a perfect pumpkin!

I was given the same opportunity when I was 28 years old. 28! Someone put a brush in my hand and I started painting. Was it good? GOSH NO! It was horrid. She never said a thing about the quality of my work. She just encouraged me to paint.

What an amazing gift she gave me.

I want to give you the same gift.

Pick up a pen, pencil or a sharpie and just doodle.

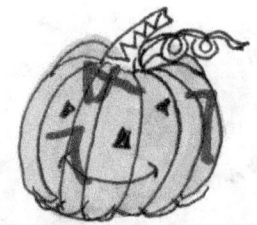

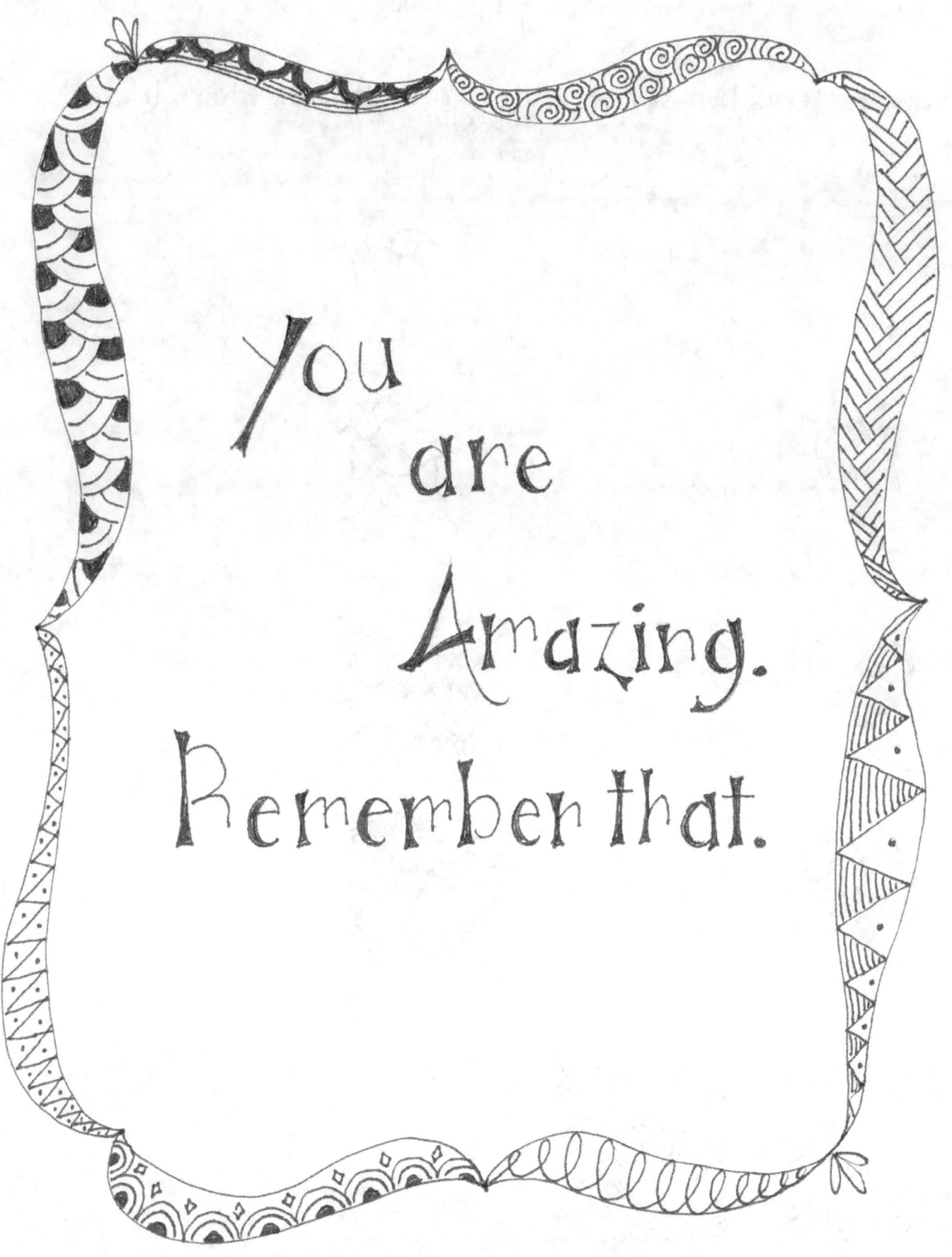

You are Amazing. Remember that.

Let's get tricky...

Some patterns look so complicated, you don't know where to start.

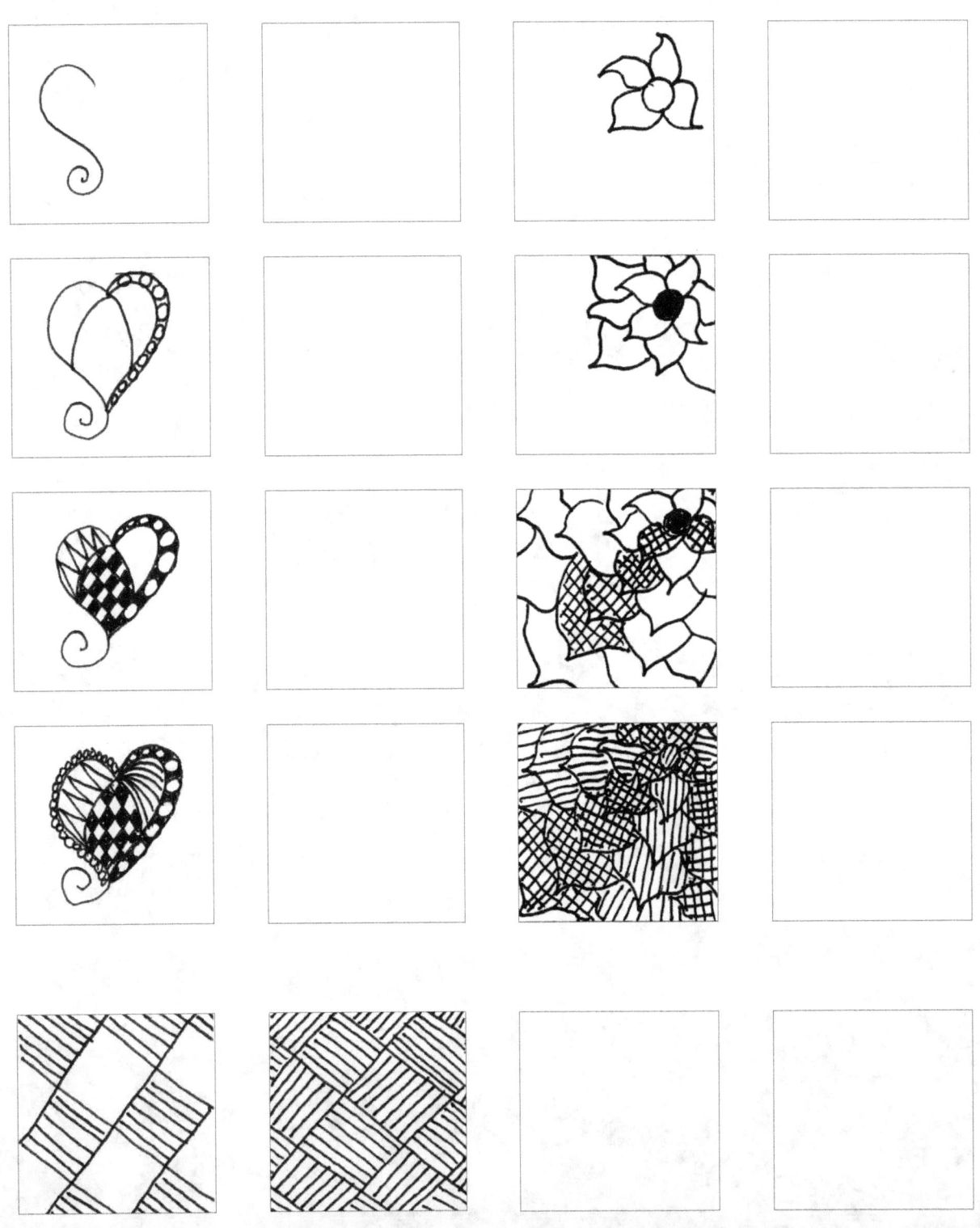

Let's get tricky again...

One step at a time...

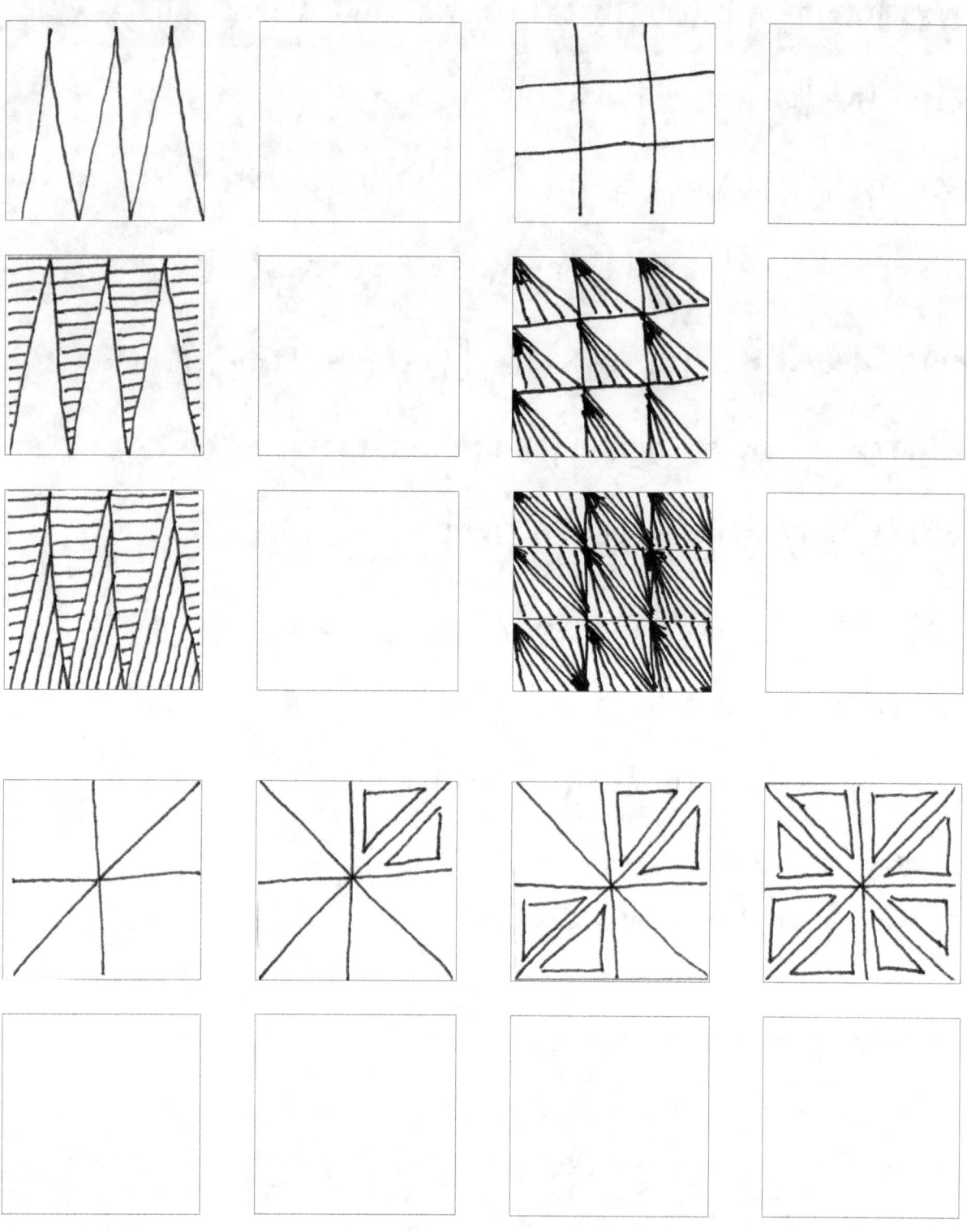

After several days of horrible △, I was discouraged.

Then my friend called.

She was having a hard time. Life was not going well.

I was looking for a way to encourage her.

I picked up the pen and started with the border.

The △ came out pretty good, so I persisted.

I browsed online for a song lyric. (Bob Marley, of course!)

Then I browsed online again for cool lettering.

The words were done in pencil first.

Then traced over with marker.

My △ was getting better again!

While trying to encourage another,

I was encouraged!

(That's the way it always works, isn't it?)

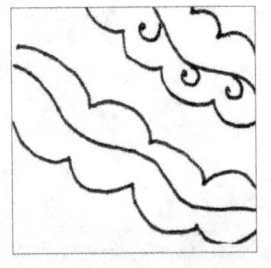 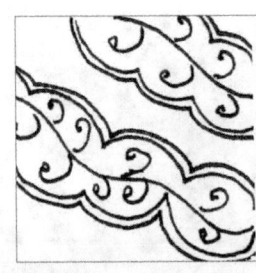  

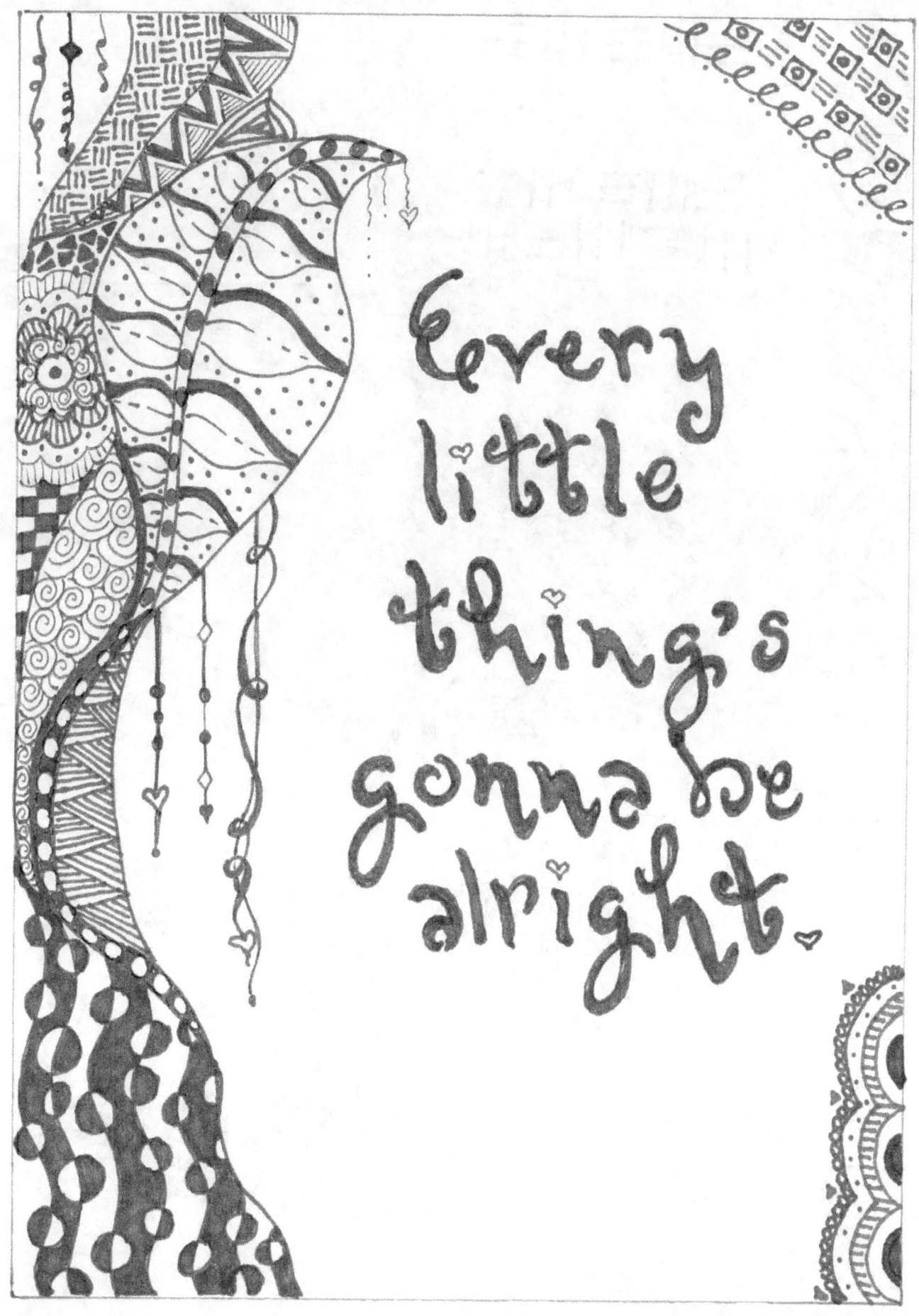

Every little thing's gonna be alright.

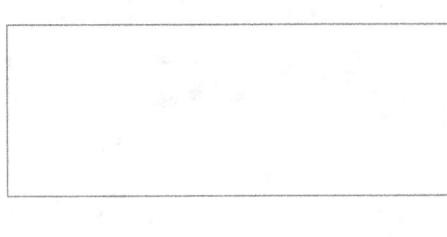

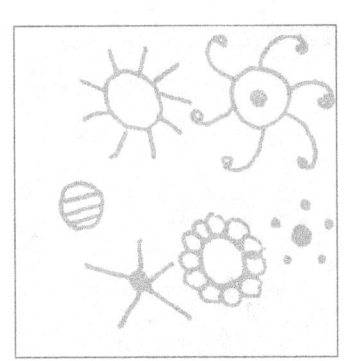

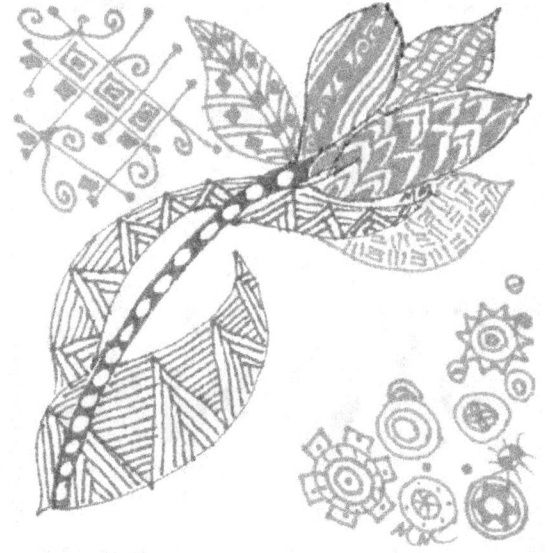

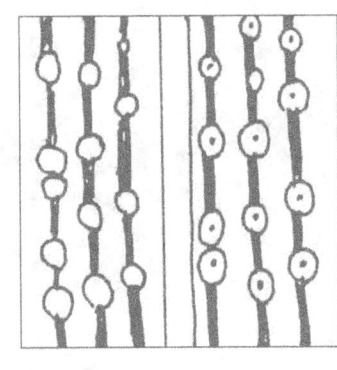

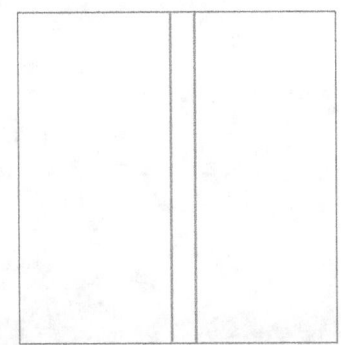

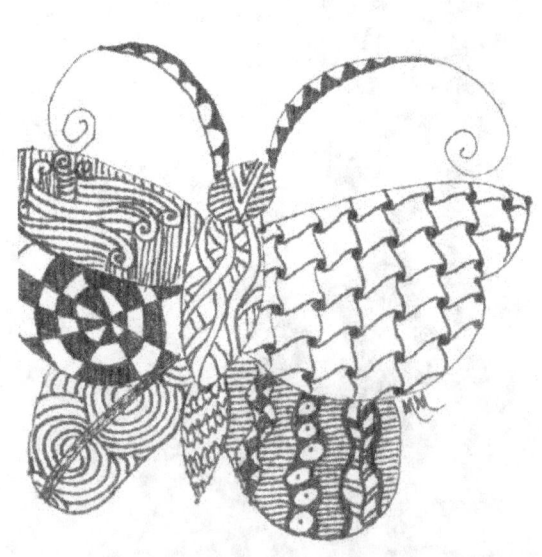

Thank you Cindy for two changes that made this book even better.

EVERYONE can !

 can inspire you, help you heal, grow, and relax.

 helps you SLOW DOWN. (Don't you hate when people tell you that?)

Please know, I am not telling you to slow down,

I am saying it can help you do it on your own.

Drawing can be meditative. For me, it might be a song lyric, favorite line from a poem or a bible verse I focus on, for you it might be quotes or lyrics or your goals and dreams.

You pick.

As you are , clear your mind.

When you find it wandering, just bring it back and focus on your idea.

Sometimes check examples on the other pages for ideas.

Sometimes DON'T.

Sometimes use a pen or paintbrush or marker.

Sometimes use all three!

There is no right or wrong.

Speaking of right and wrong...

MISKATES.

Making them, Repeating them, Learning from them...

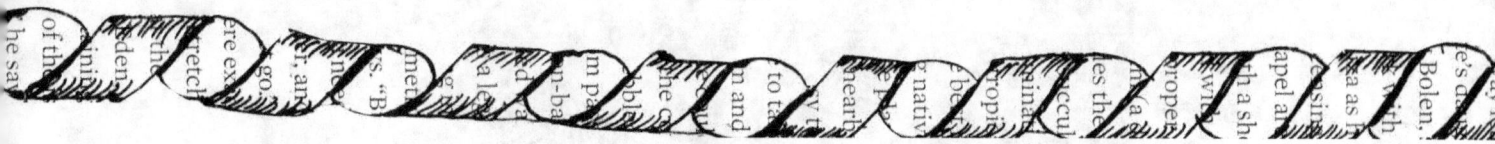

Make miskates.

Miskates are what you make along the way...

And when you get there, guess what?
You will make more!

Miskates do NOT define you, they help you grow!

(As a person and an artist!)

YOU WILL CONTINUE TO MAEK MISTAKES,

JUST NOT THE SAME ONES...

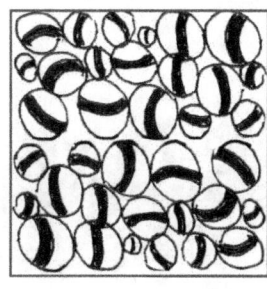 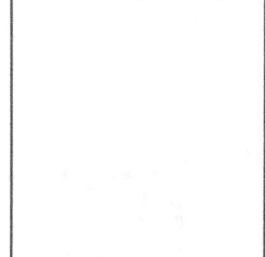

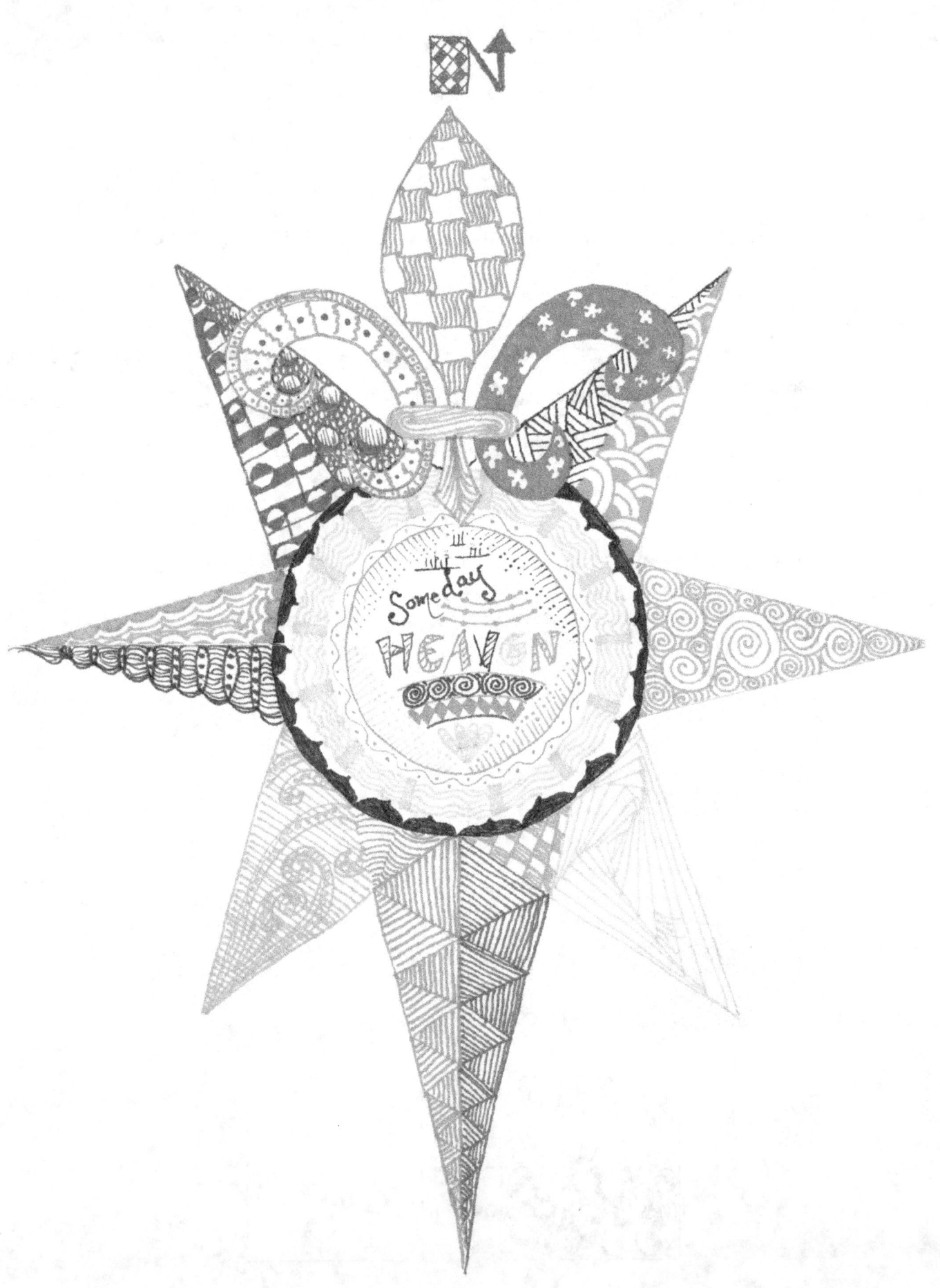

Doodle Me This

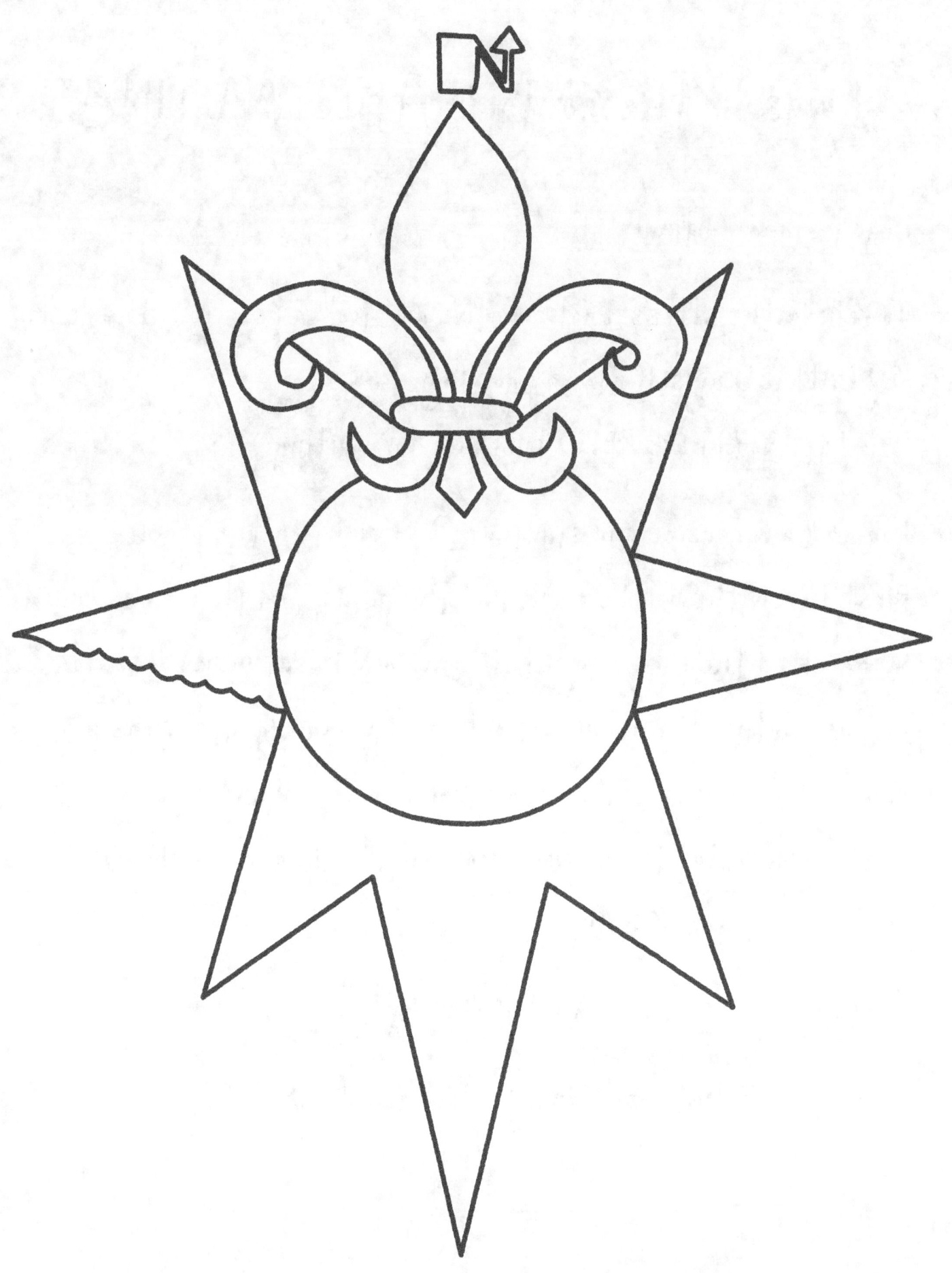

I was in the doctor's office WAITING.

I can't stand waiting!

To relieve the stress, I got creative and took a pen from the desk and CALMED myself down by doodling.
(Did I tell you I have ZERO tolerance for waiting?)

I opened a magazine and started △ - right on the page!
First, I drew the middle circle and the petals and then I was called in. I grabbed the page, brought it home and it sat in my desk for over a month. Then I pulled it out one day and added just one new doodle. I put it away again. Each stage looked cool and I thought it was complete, but then I would look at it again and I would add another △ and VOILA!!

Pretty cool AND looks impossible, right?

Look at each doodle individually, most are VERY EASY.

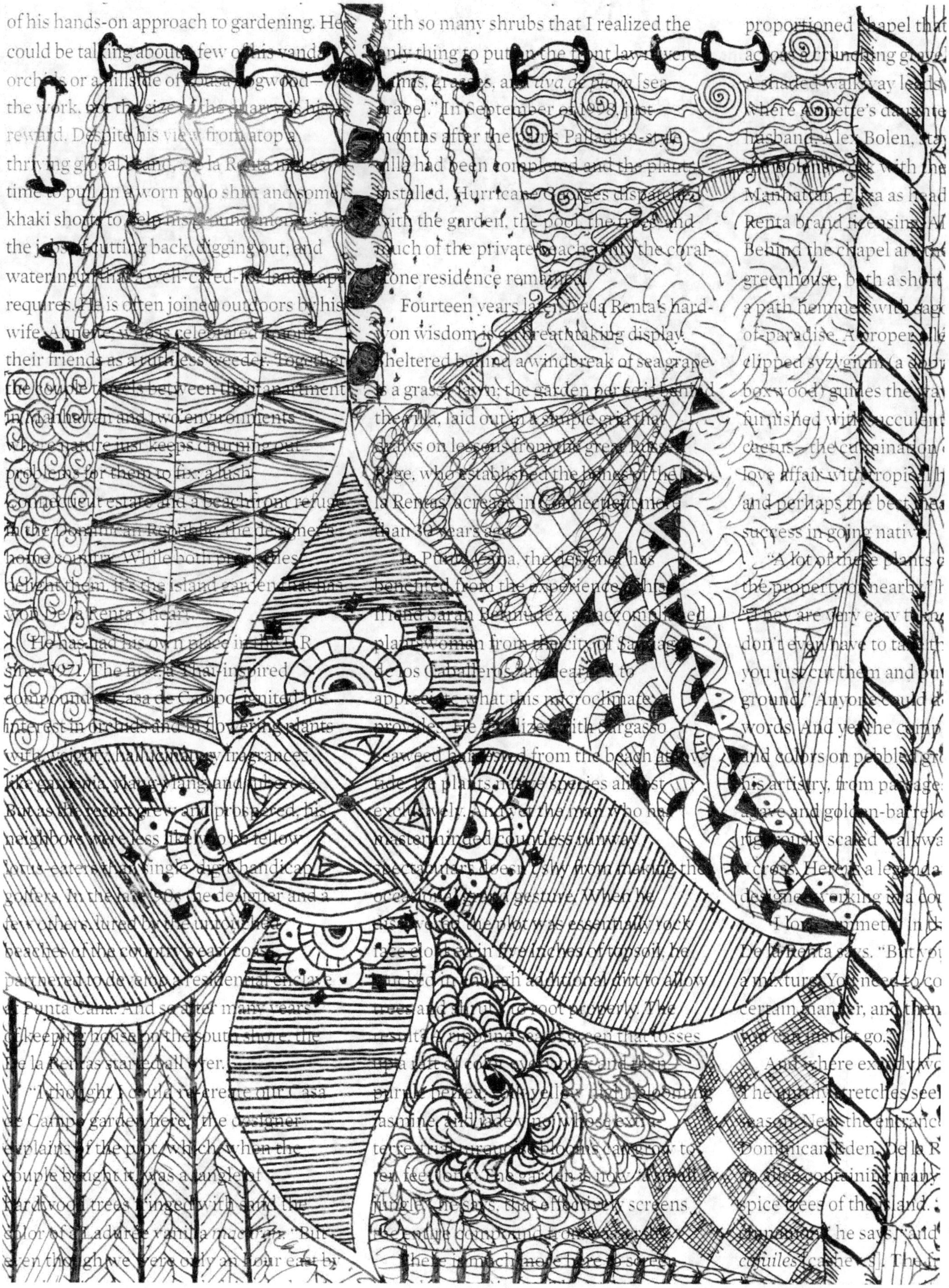

Have pen, will doodle!

I doodled this while talking to my friend one day. On the back of a random piece of paper.

Took it home redrew it and created a picture for my daughter's dorm room.

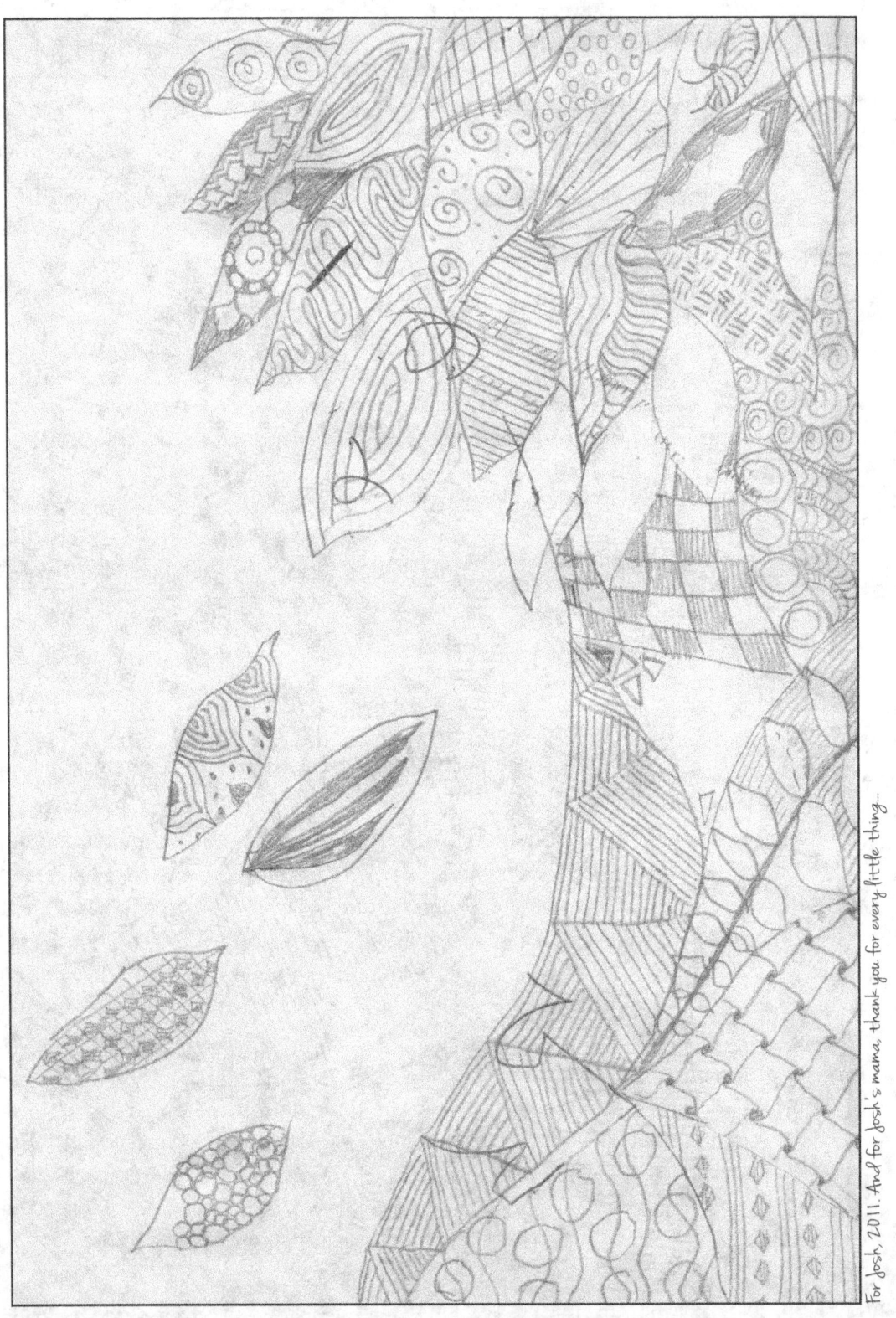

For Josh, 2011. And for Josh's mama, thank you for every little thing...

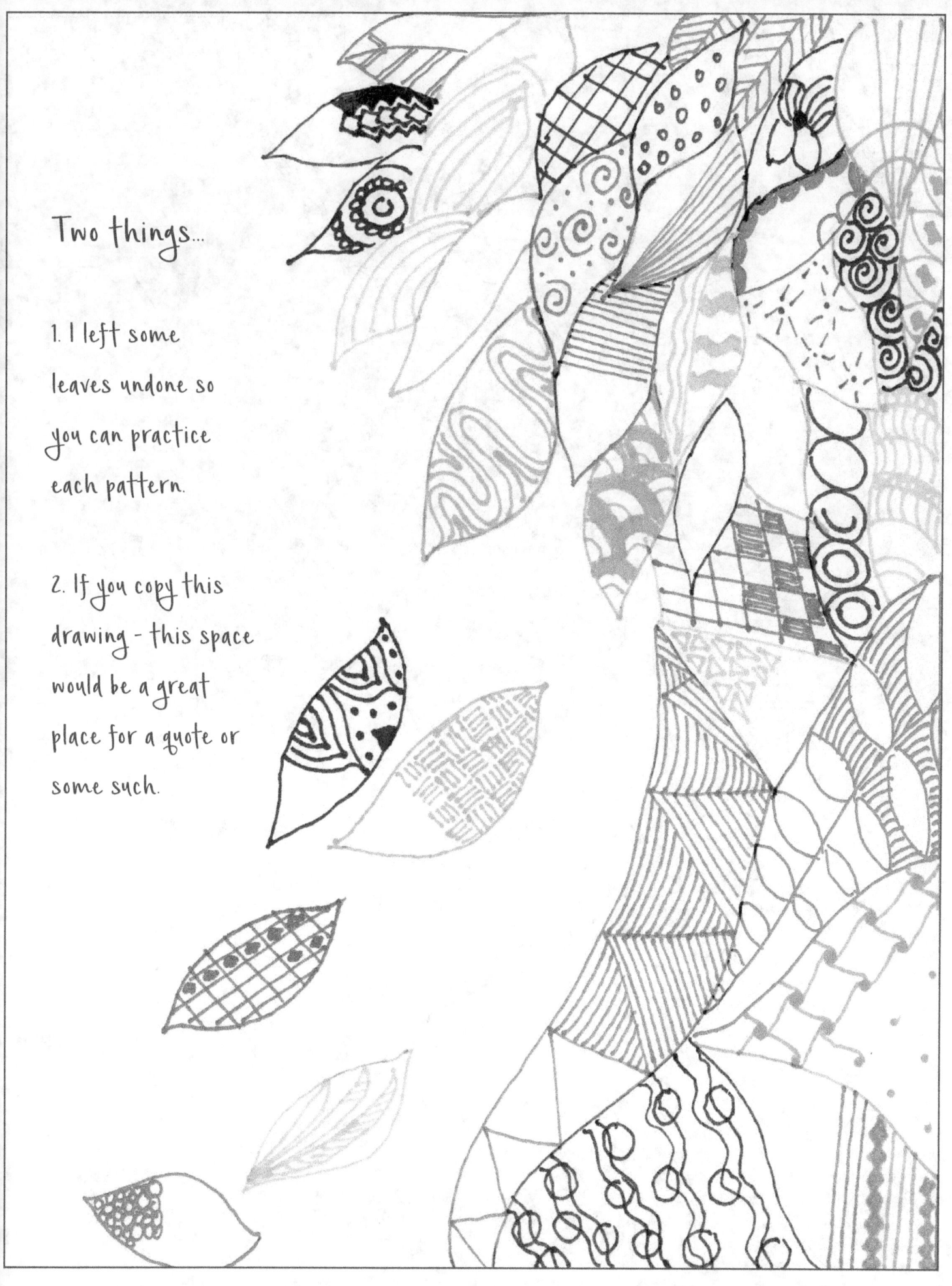

Two things...

1. I left some
leaves undone so
you can practice
each pattern.

2. If you copy this
drawing - this space
would be a great
place for a quote or
some such.

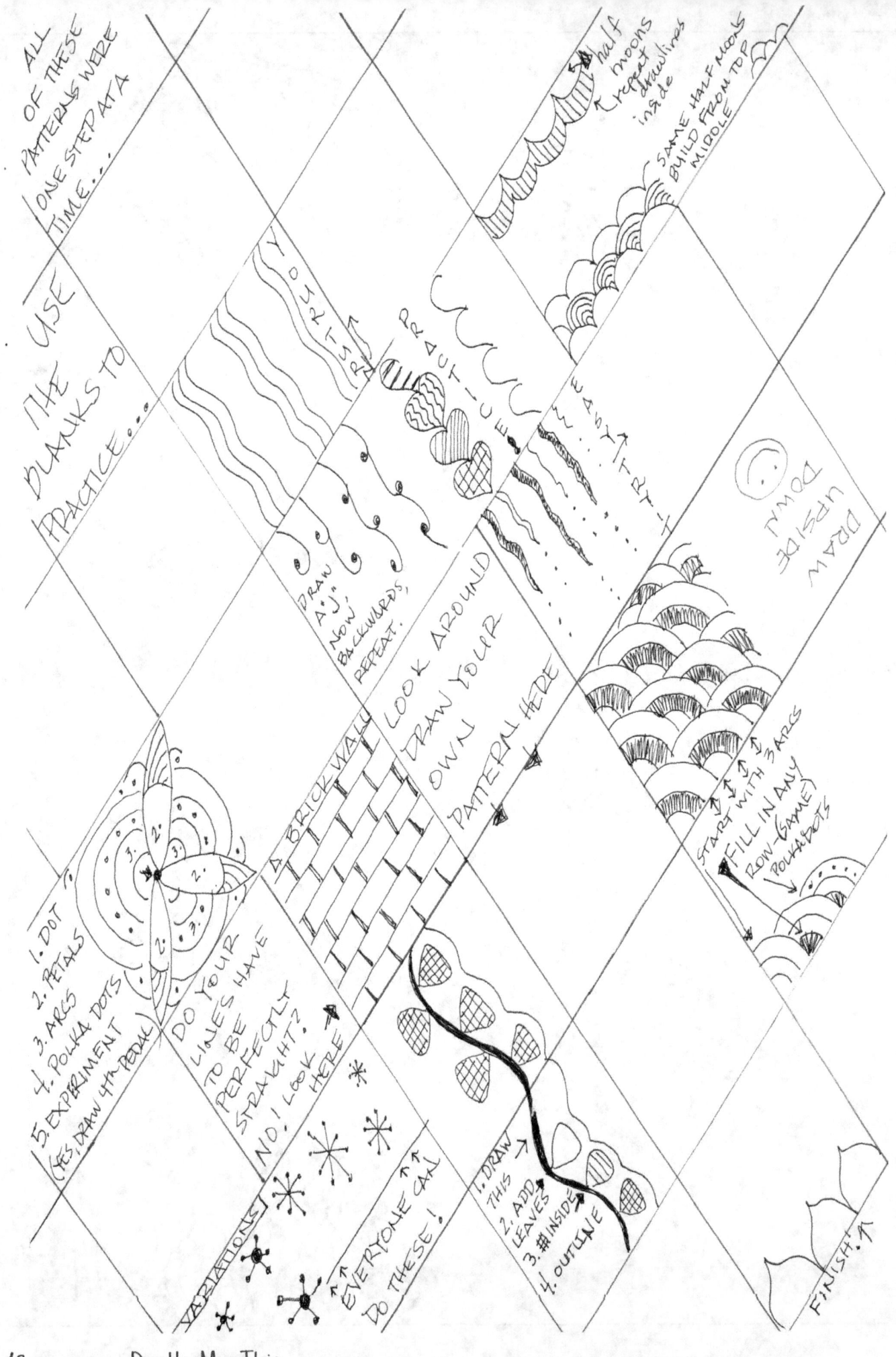

ALL OF THESE PATTERNS WERE ONE STEP AT A TIME...

USE THE BLANKS TO PRACTICE...

half moons (repeat drawings inside)

SAME HALF MOONS BUILD FROM TOP MIDDLE

PRACTICE

EASY PATTERNS

DRAW A "J", NOW BACKWARDS, REPEAT.

DRAW UPSIDE DOWN

LOOK AROUND DRAW YOUR OWN PATTERN HERE

FILL IN ANY ROW (SAME) POLKA DOTS

START WITH 3 ARCS

A BRICK WALL

1. DOT
2. PETALS
3. ARCS
4. POLKA DOTS
5. EXPERIMENT
(YES, DRAW 4th PEDAL)

DO YOUR LINES HAVE TO BE PERFECTLY STRAIGHT? NO! LOOK HERE

VARIATIONS

EVERYONE CAN DO THESE!

1. DRAW THIS
2. ADD LEAVES
3. # INSIDE
4. OUTLINE

FINISH

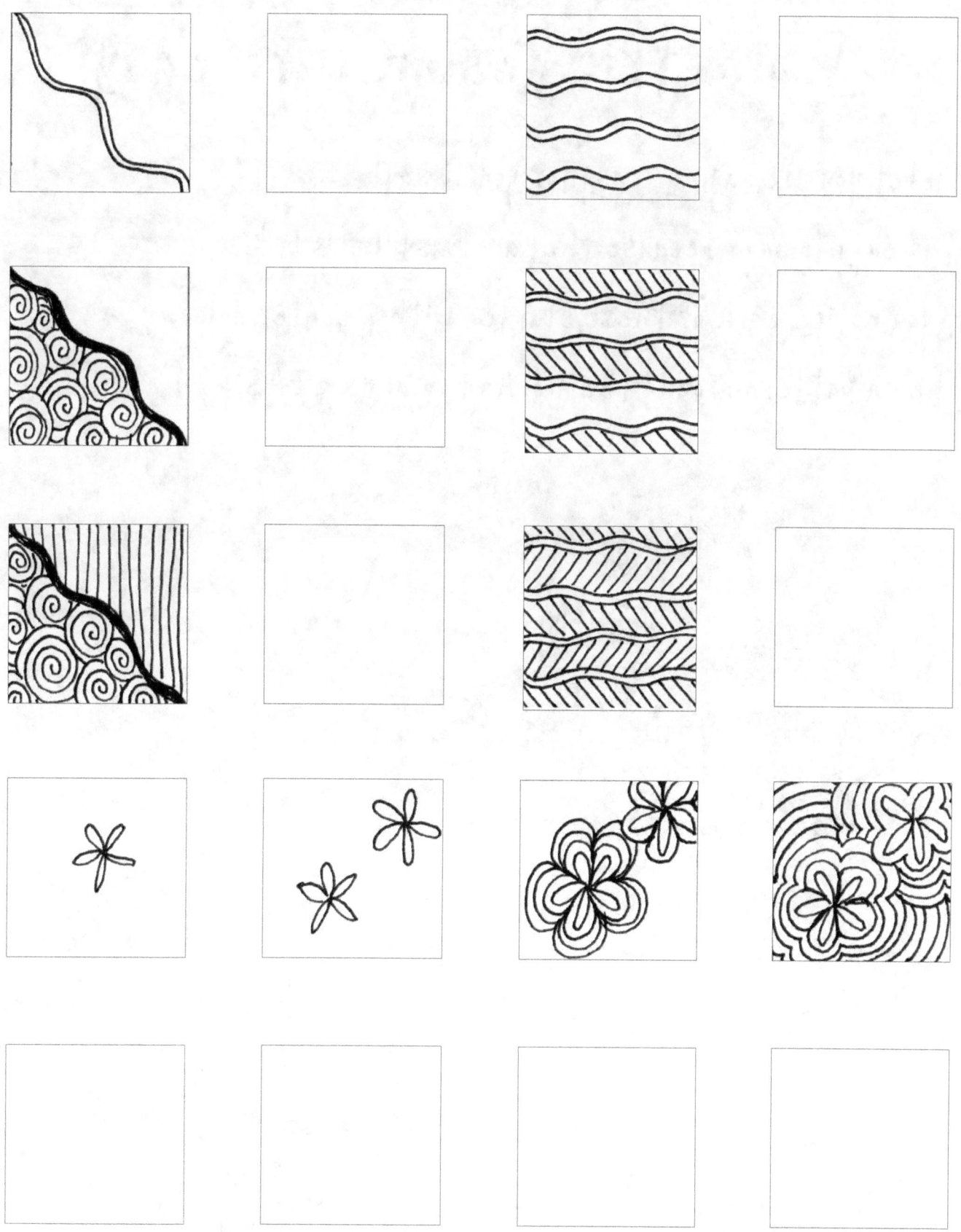

Geometric designs are easy!

I'll bet you are saying, "easy for you to say."

It is easy to say - because they are easy! Let's look...

If you notice, each of these started with a center dot.

Then a pattern around the dot. And on and on. EASY.

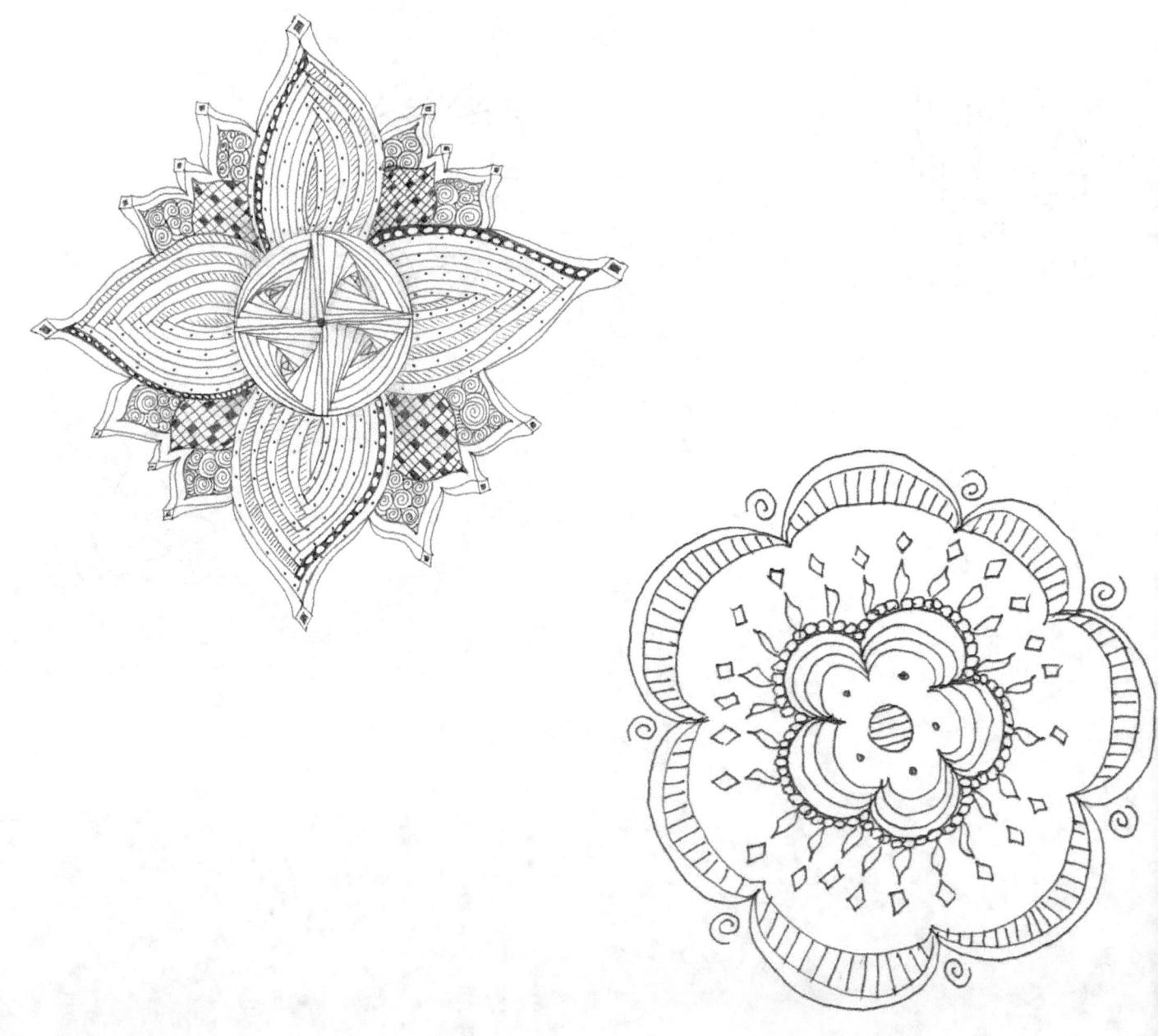

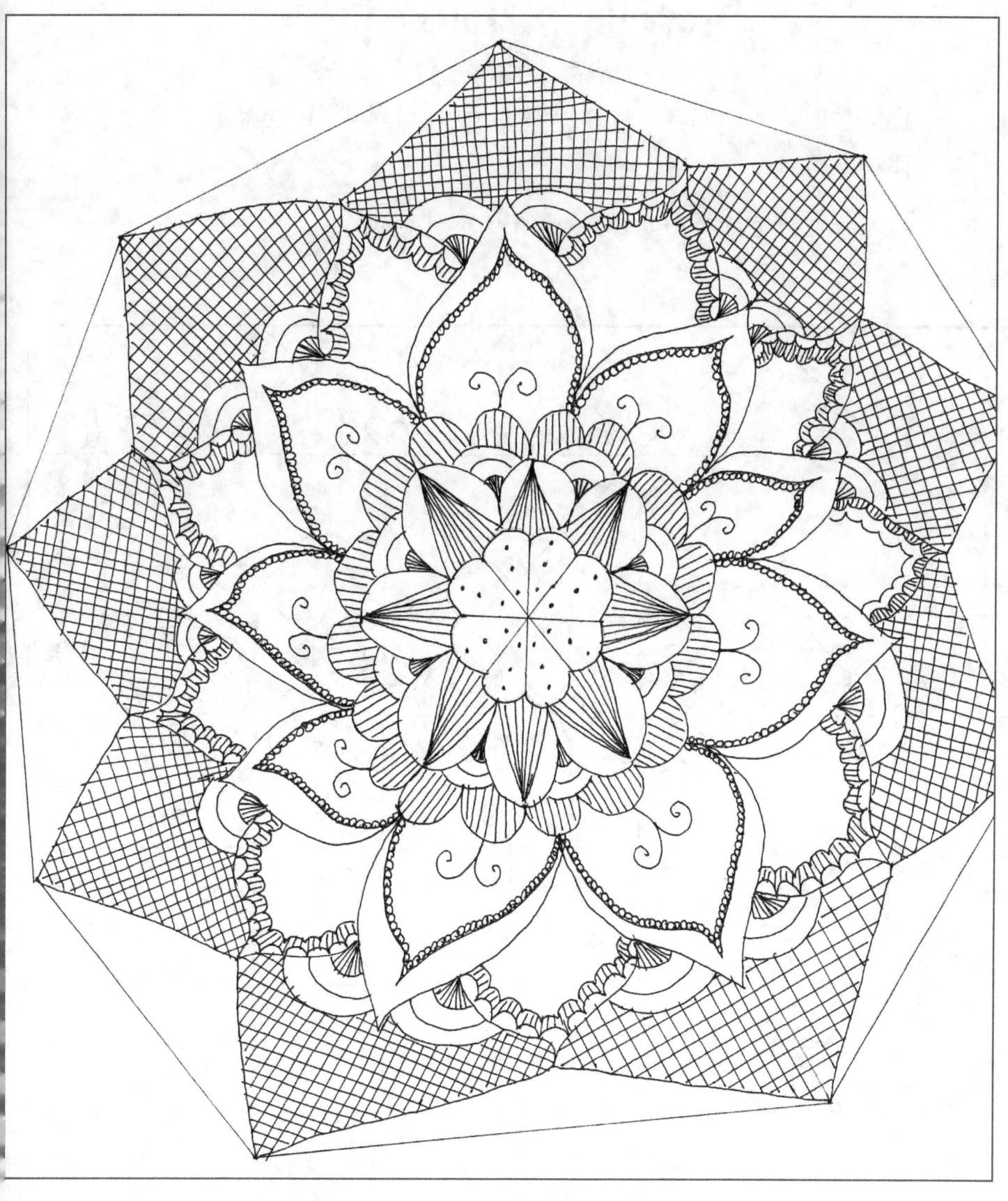

Now it's your turn!

The designs on the previous page look complicated, don't they?

They are not.

Copy each step from this page onto the next page.

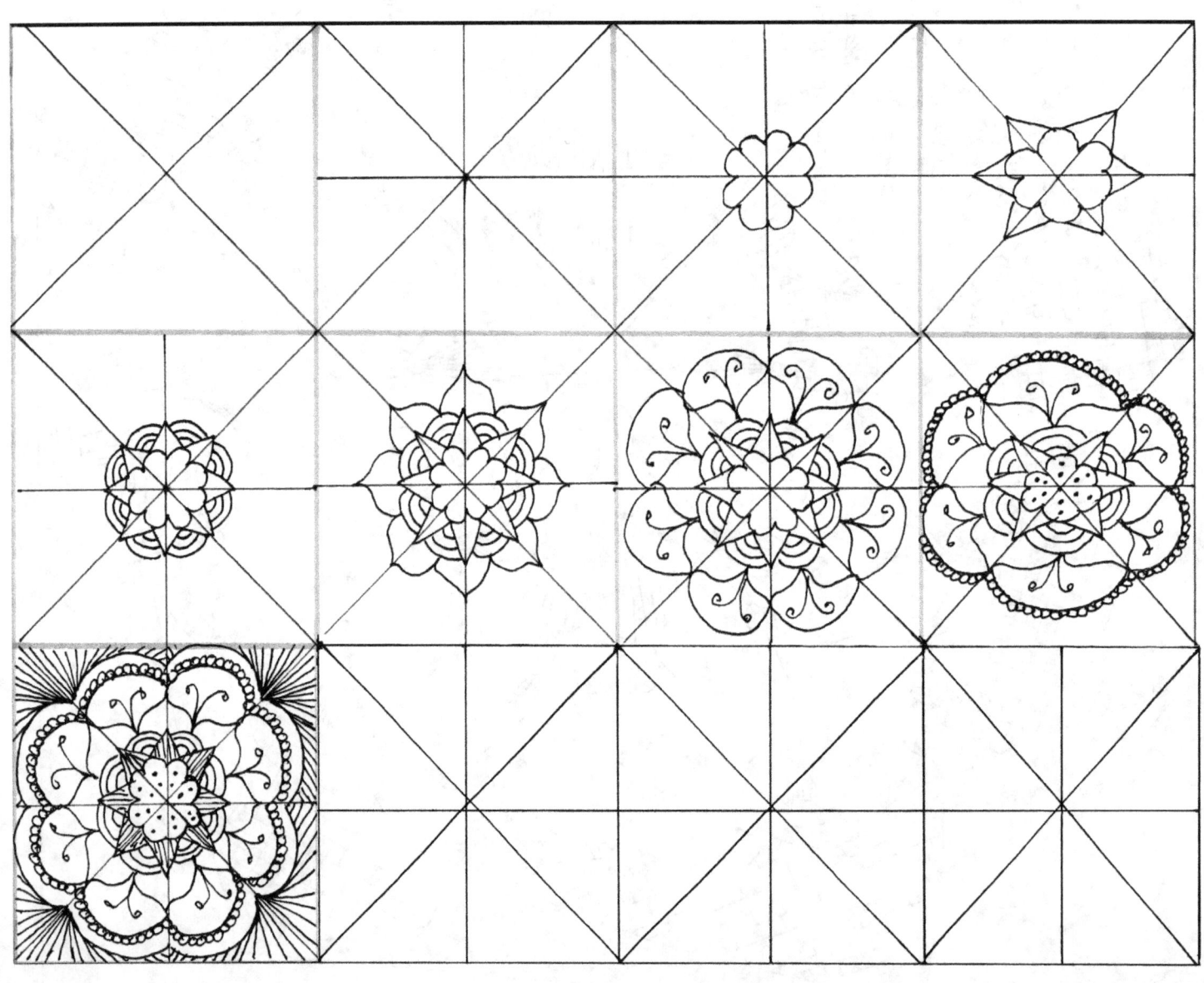

I have created the guidelines. Once you learn the pattern you will start to realize how it works. It's the same pattern over and over and over.

Fill in each box step by step.

BTW, Initially when creating your own you will start with an "X" across entire page and then a "t". And that's your template!

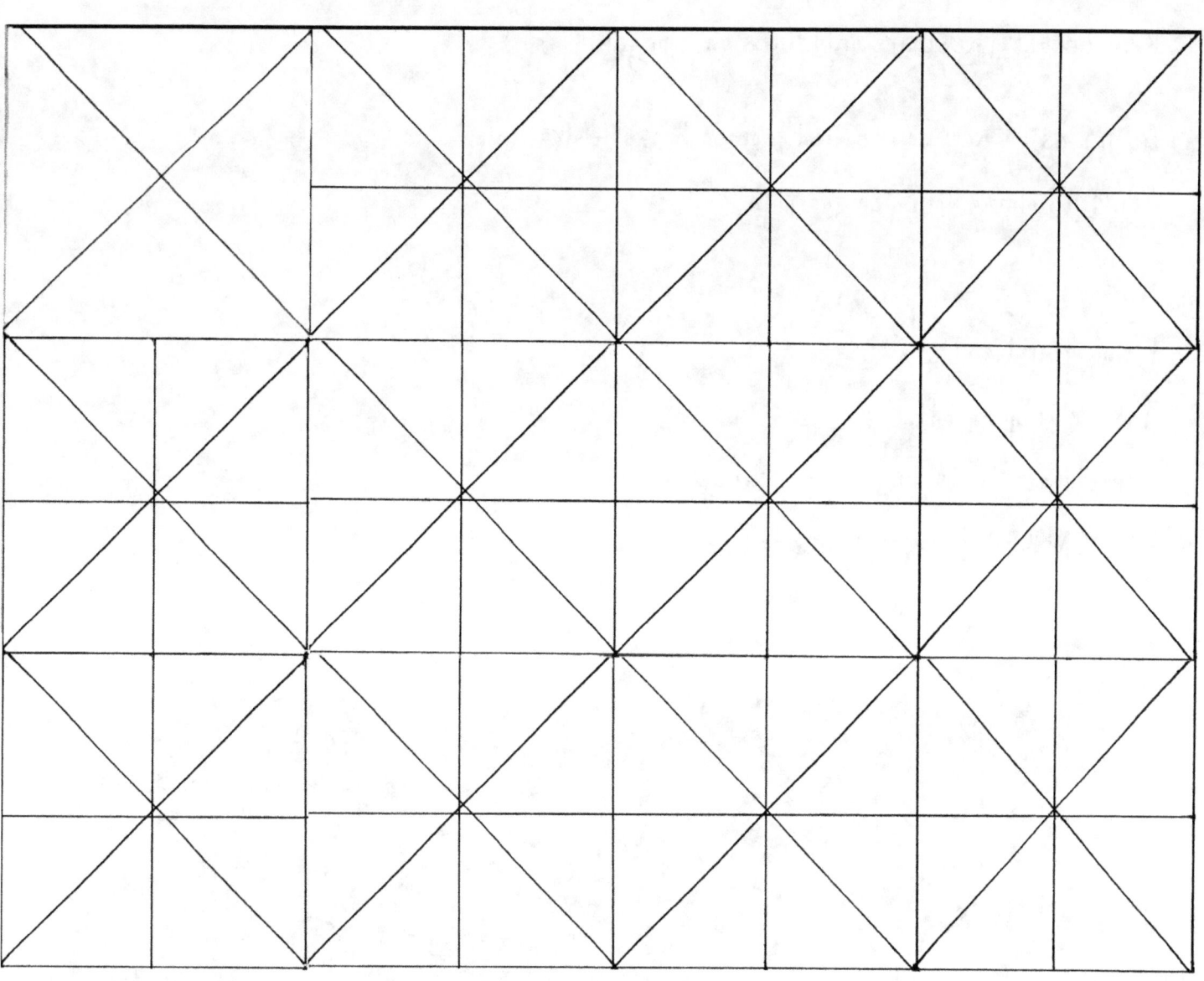

Random Thoughts.

This book is designed to create joy, peace and grace.

If it doesn't, here are some thoughts...

Done or partly done is okay!

Remember these are only lines on a page!

As far as I know no one died from a horrible drawing.

Are you holding your pen too tight?

If so:

Relax your hand.

Take a deep breath.

Sometimes focus on your breathing.

REMEMBER to relax your hand and...

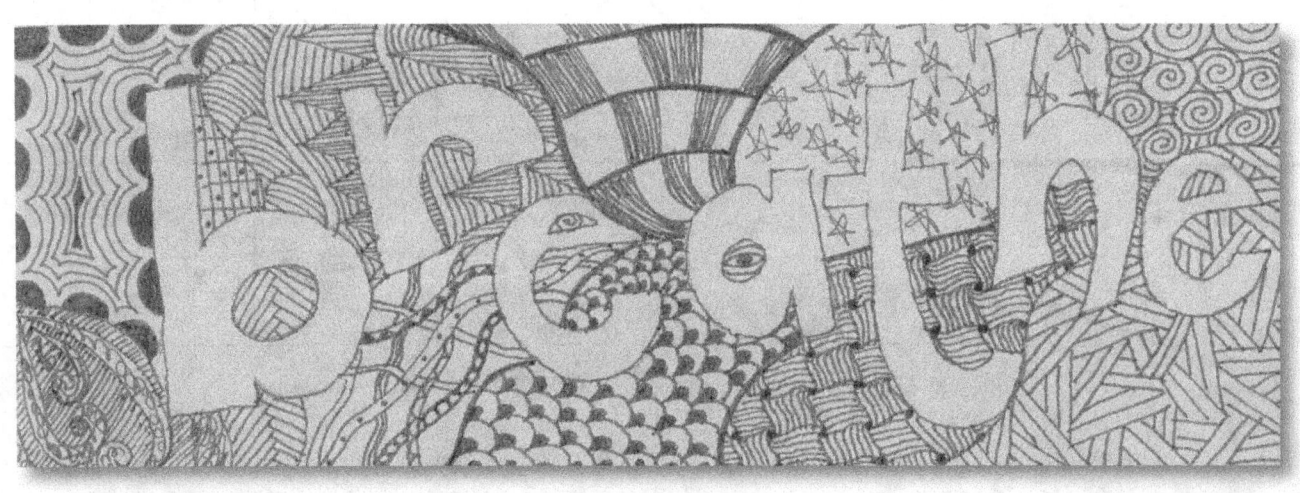

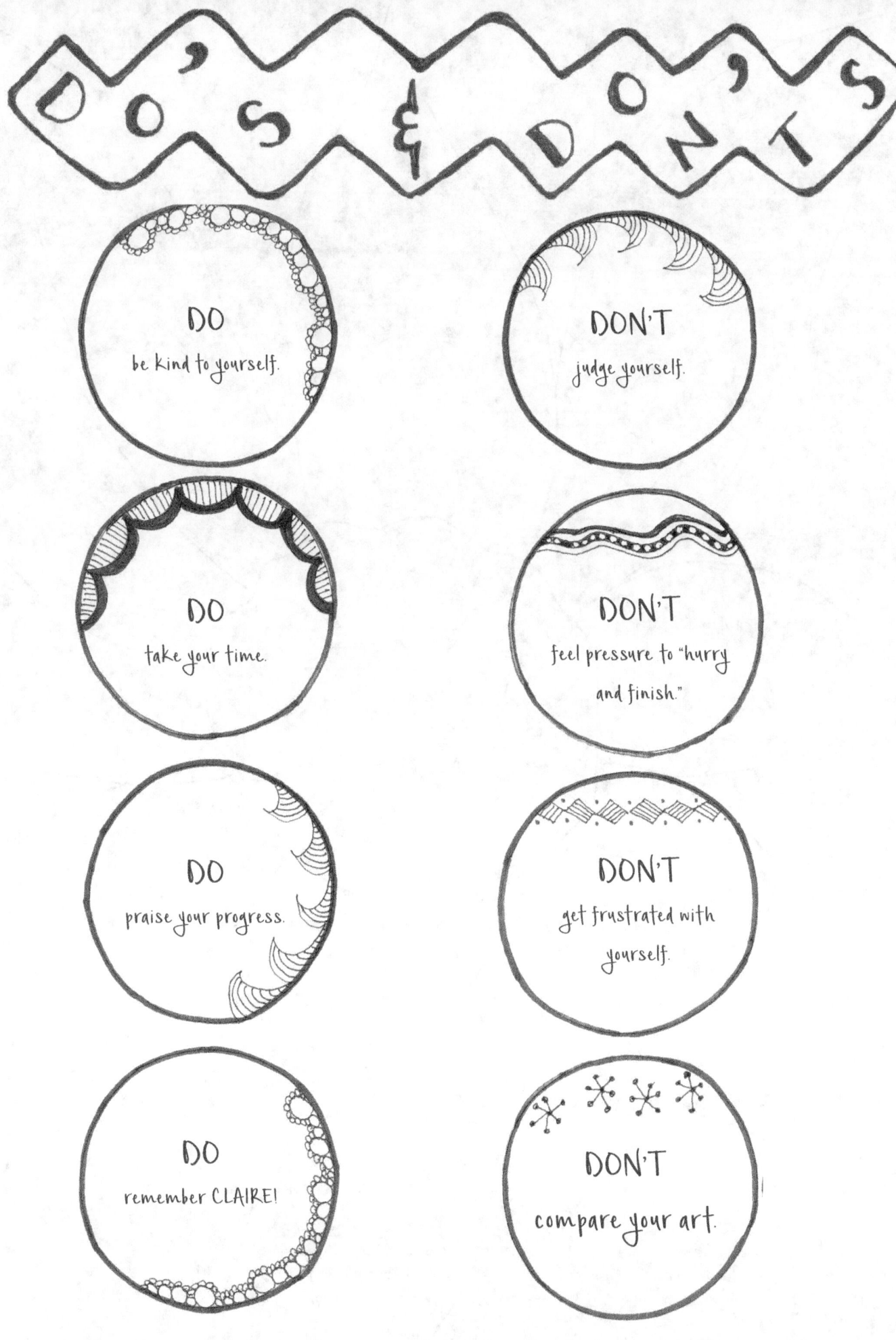

DO'S & DON'TS

DO
be kind to yourself.

DON'T
judge yourself.

DO
take your time.

DON'T
feel pressure to "hurry and finish."

DO
praise your progress.

DON'T
get frustrated with yourself.

DO
remember CLAIRE!

DON'T
compare your art.

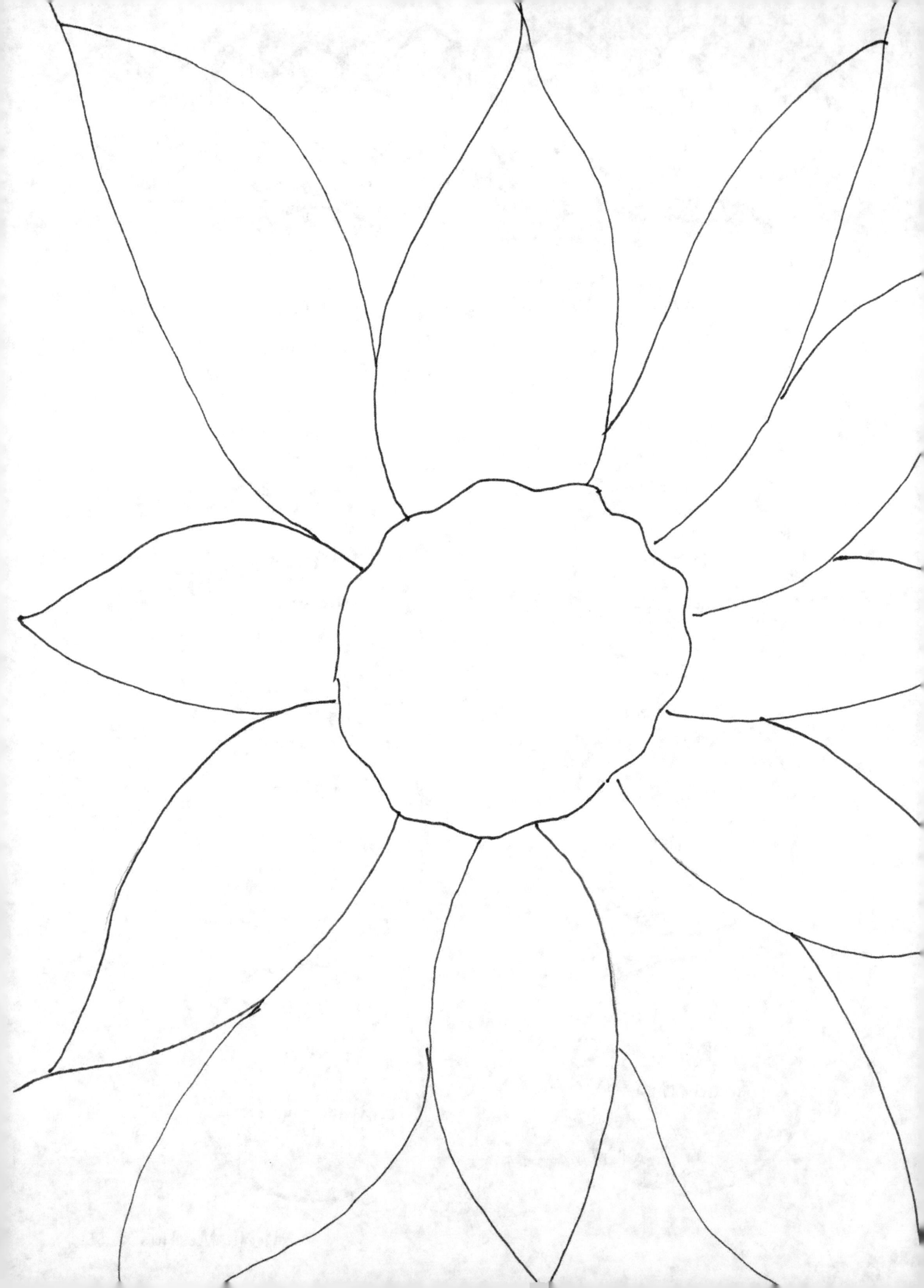

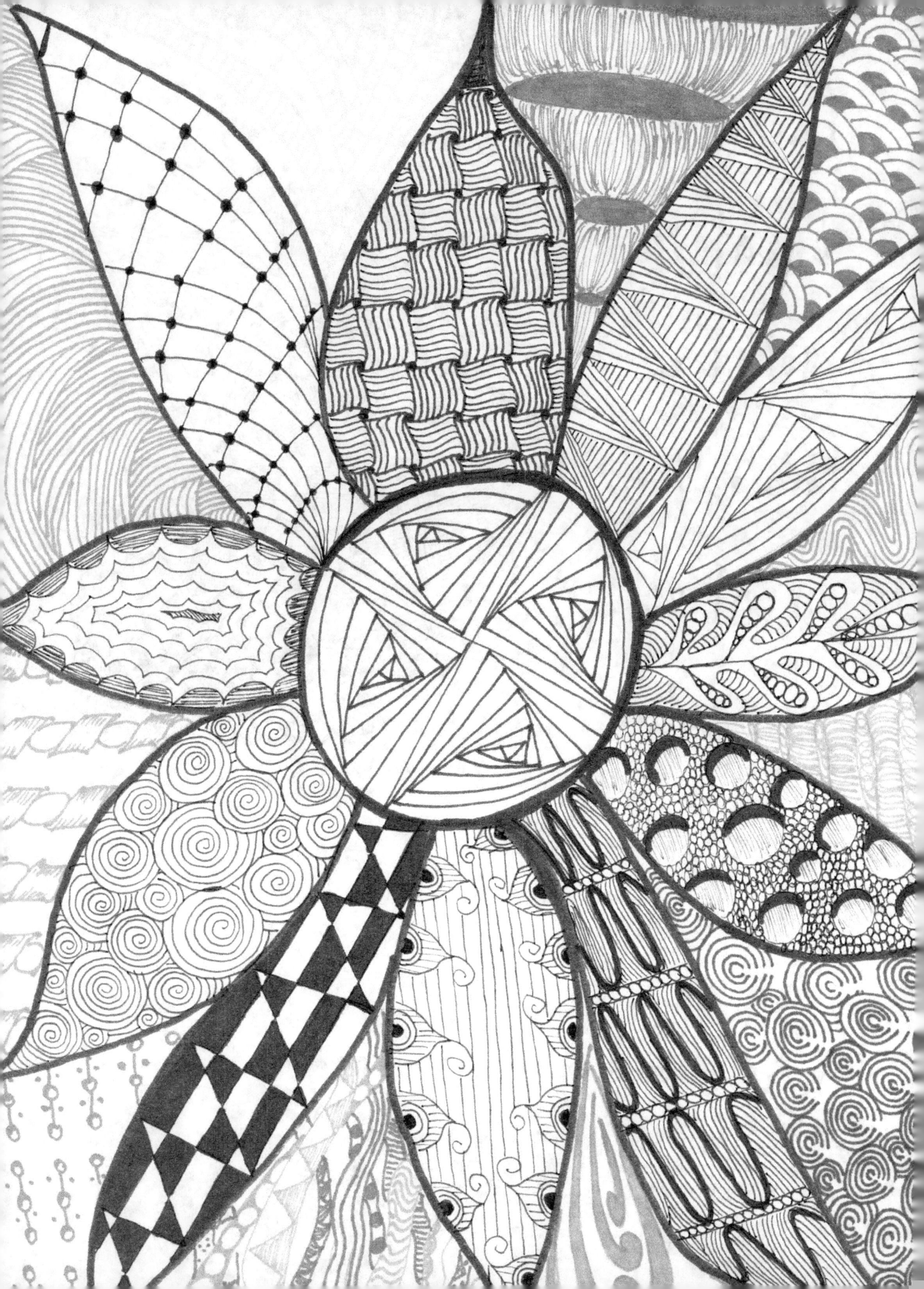

The more

creative

you are,

the more

creative

you get.

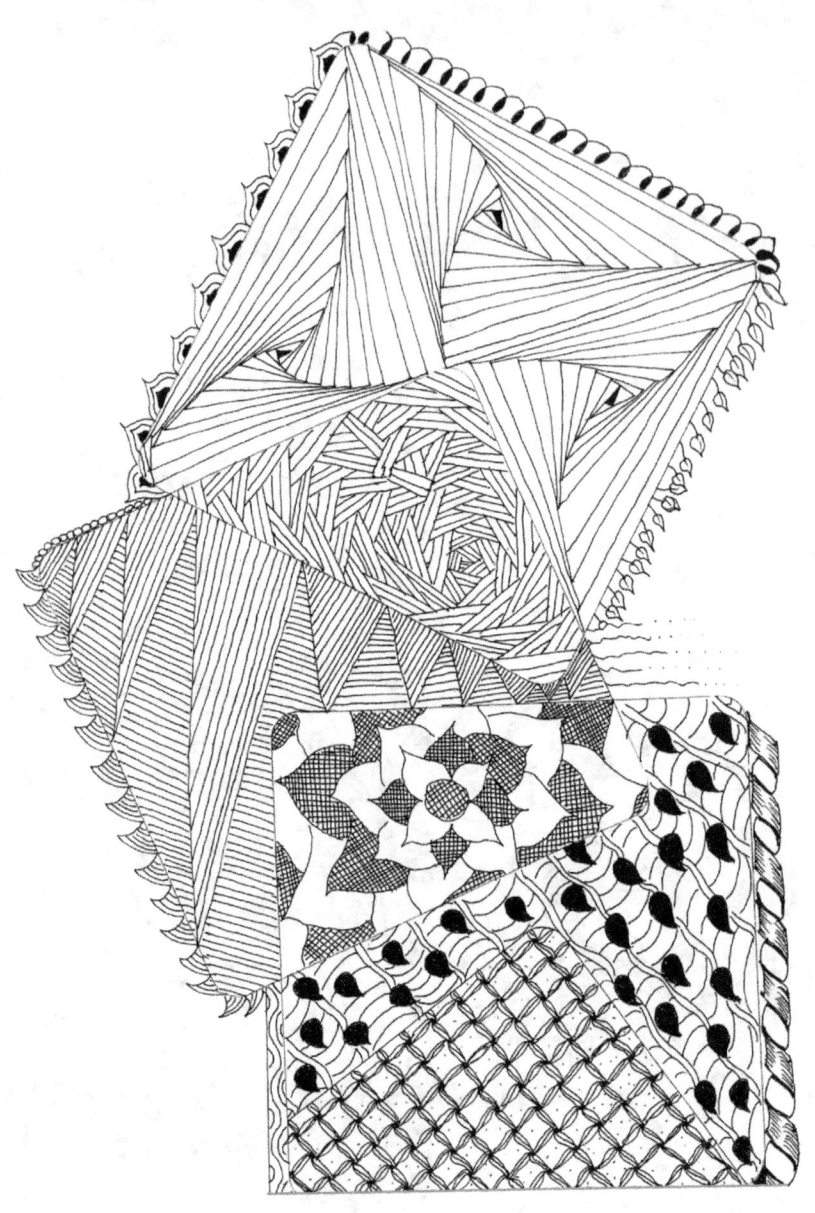

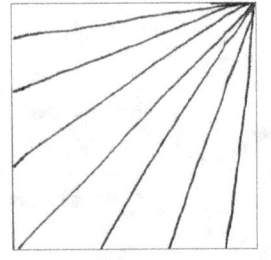

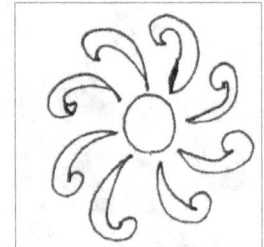

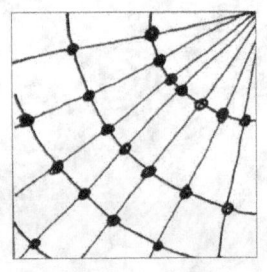

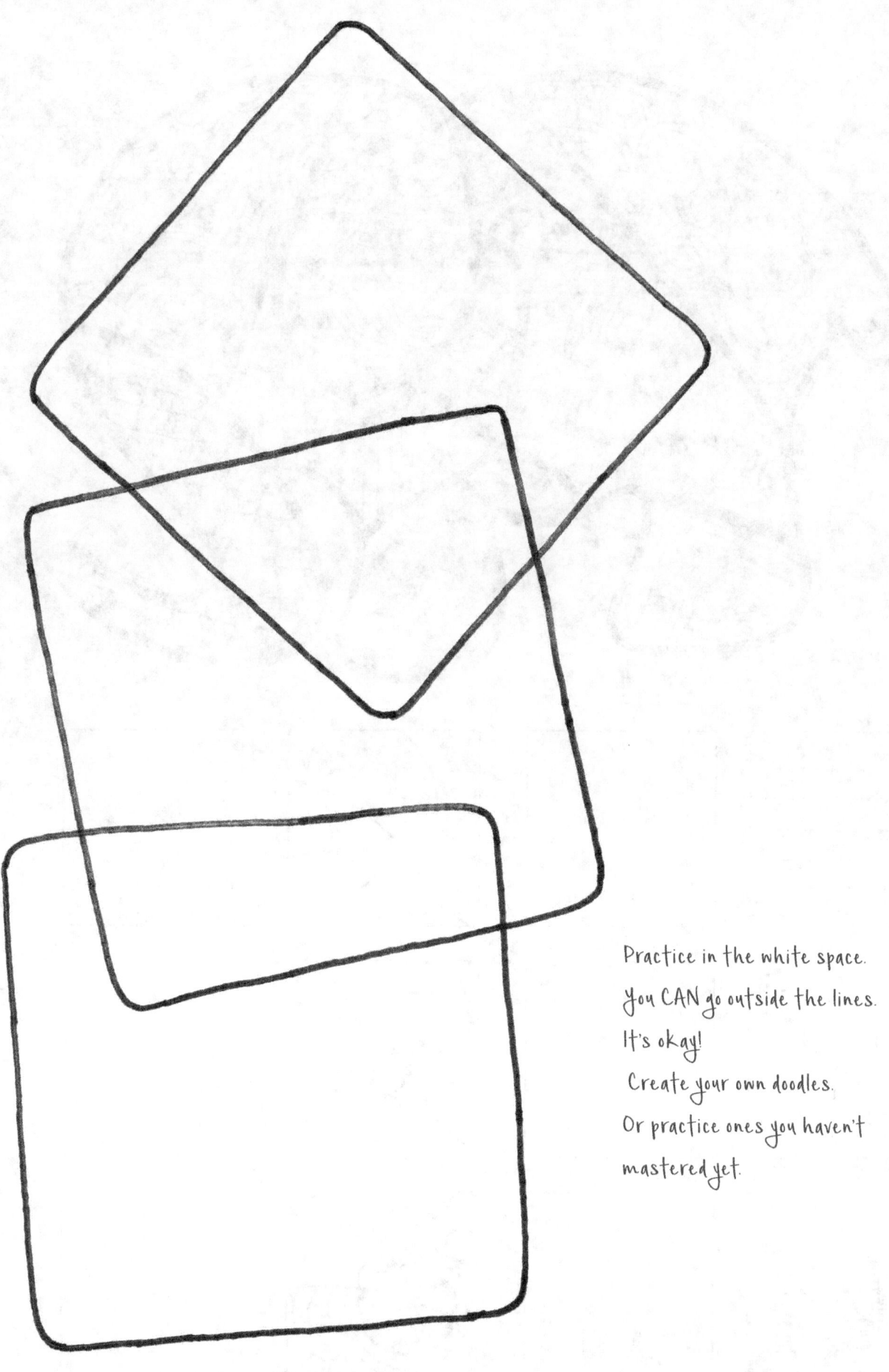

Practice in the white space.
You CAN go outside the lines.
It's okay!
Create your own doodles.
Or practice ones you haven't
mastered yet.

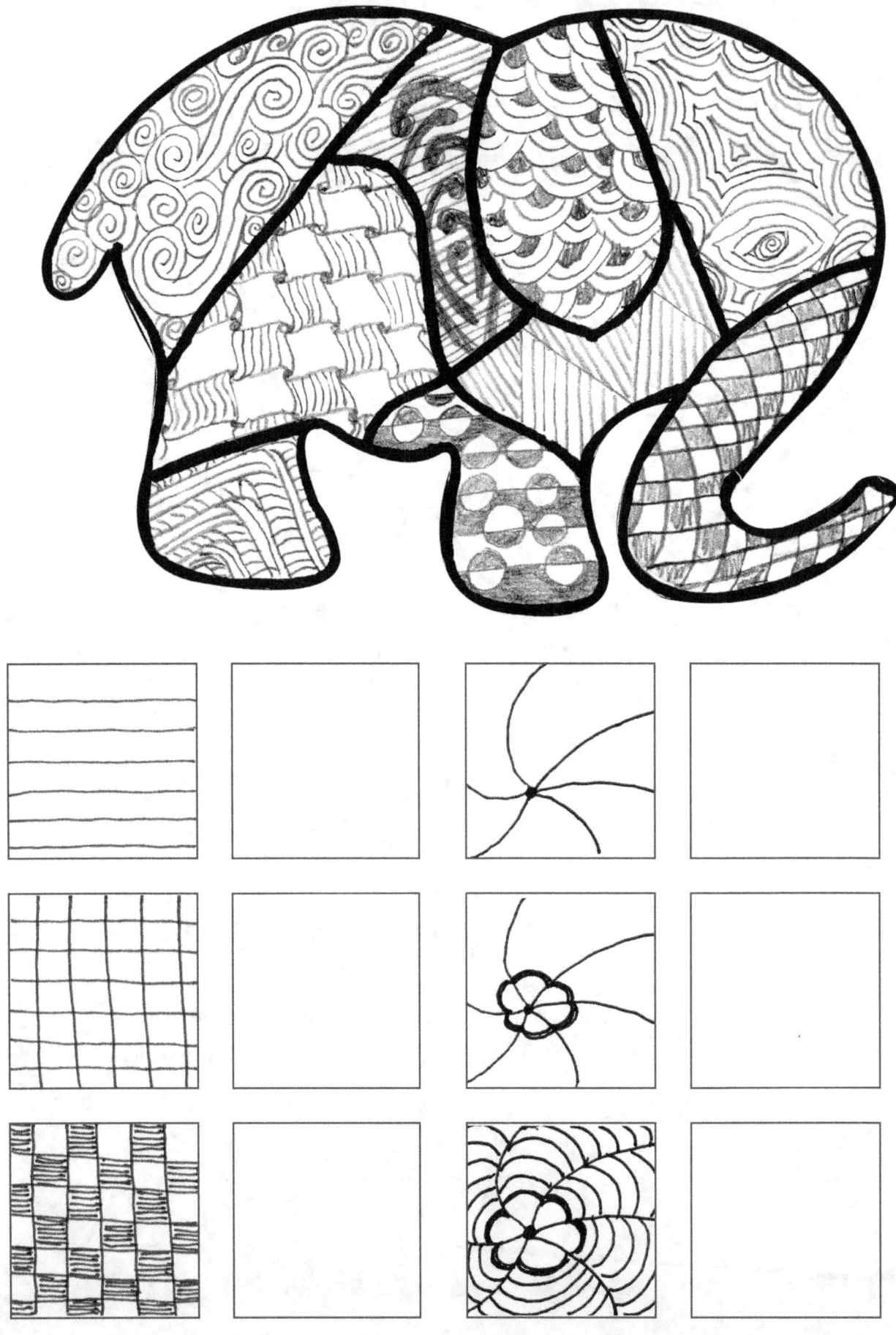

Doodle Me This

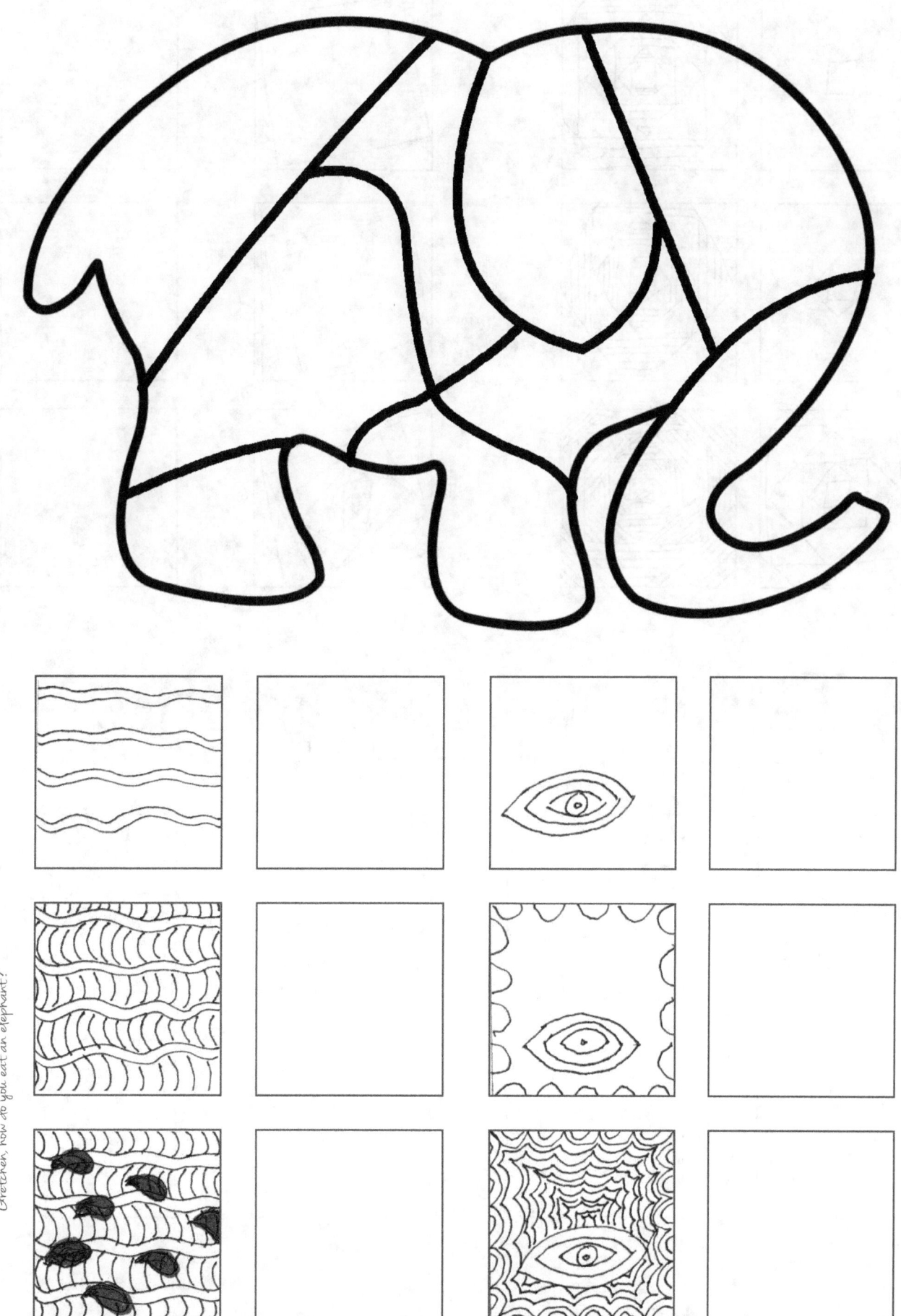

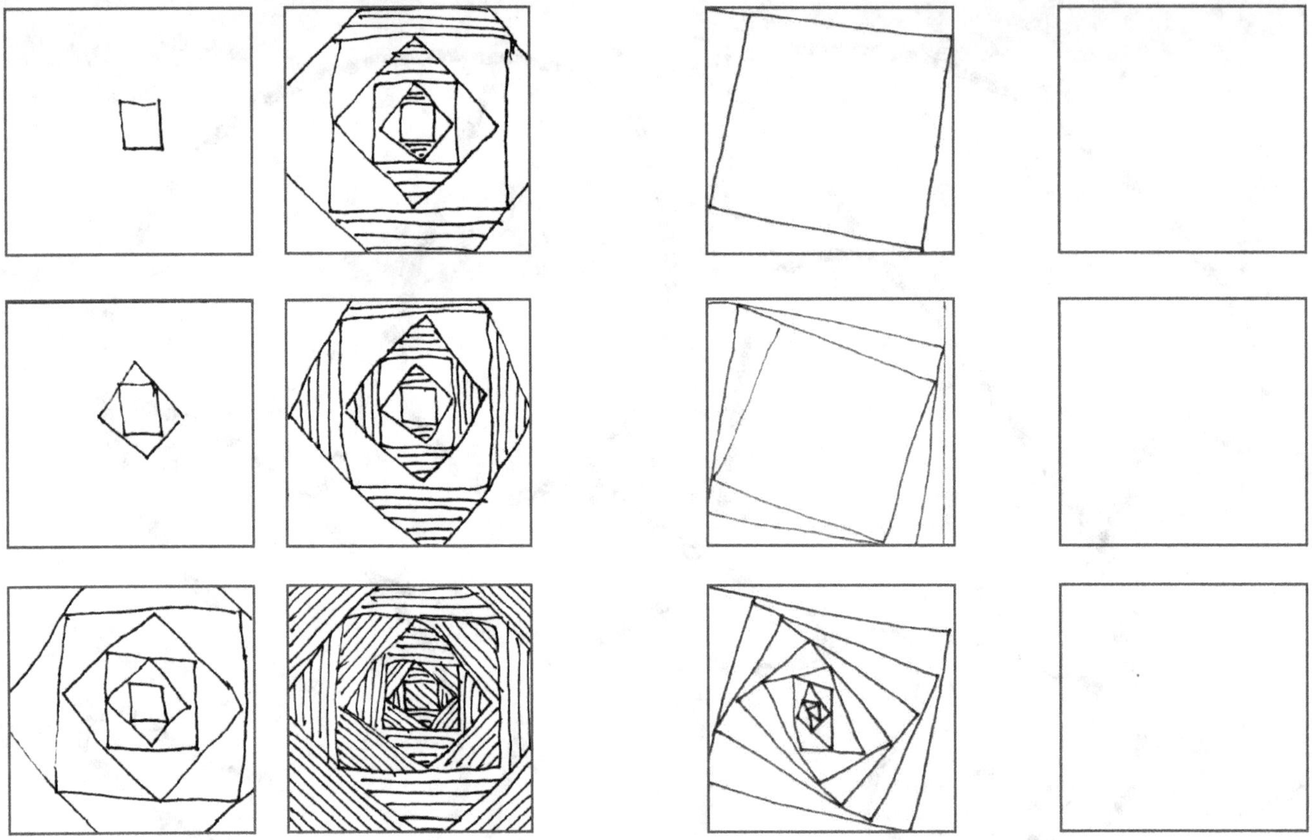

This is where we practice.

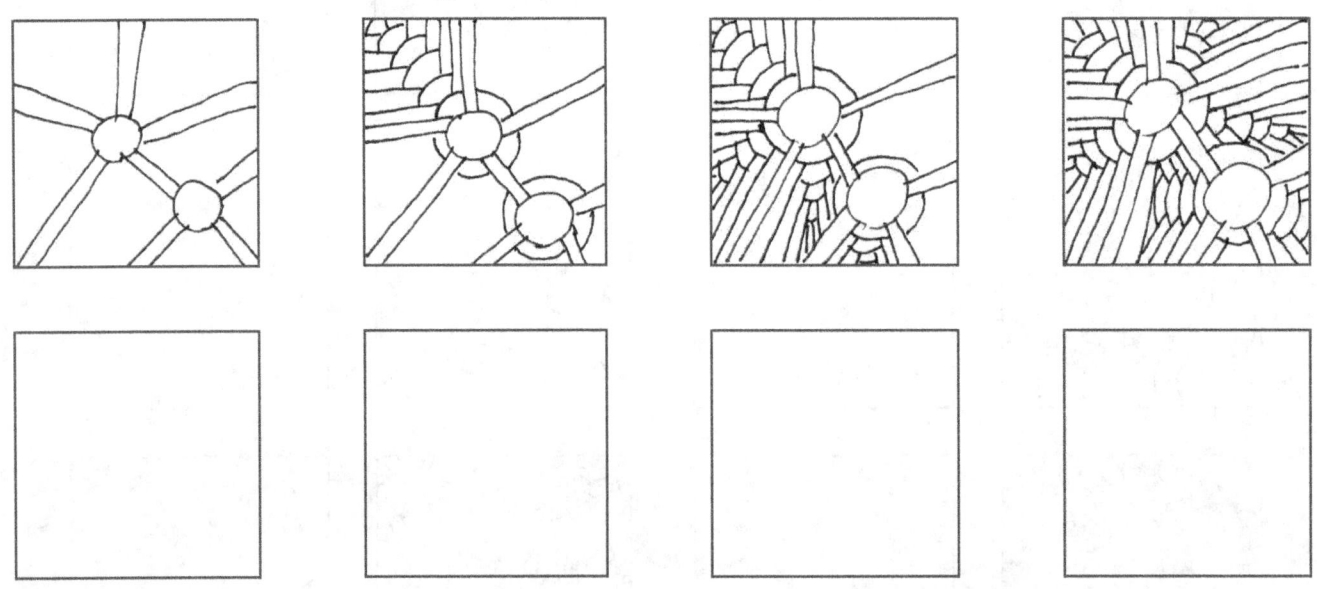

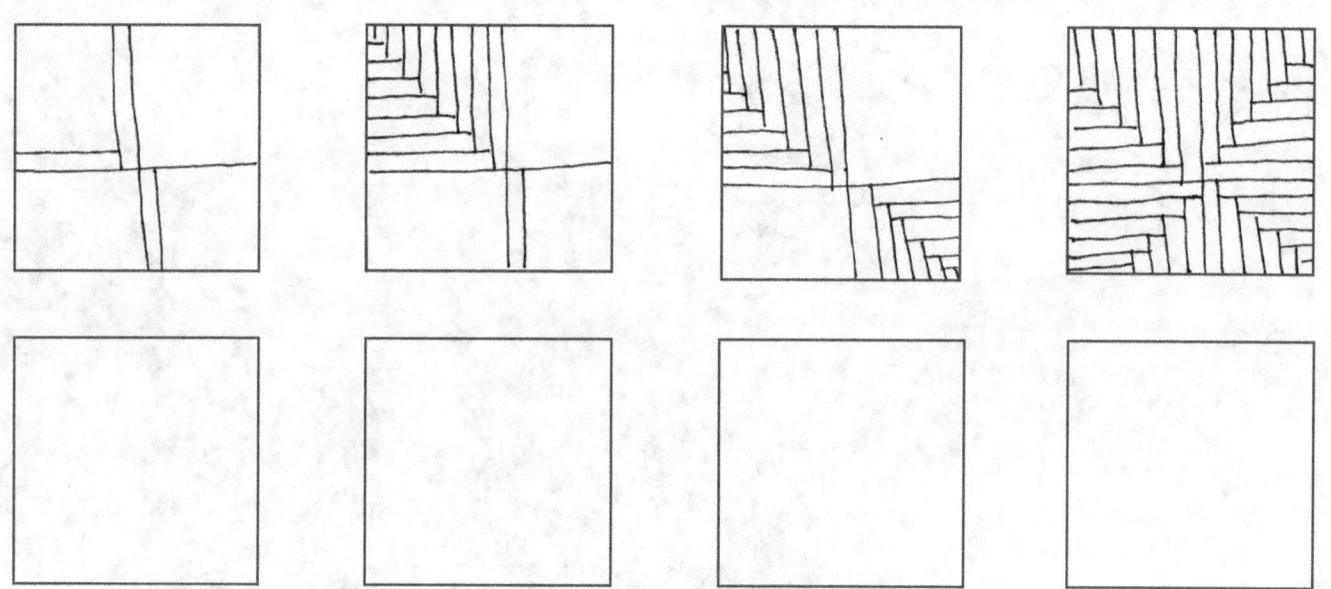

This is where we practice some more.

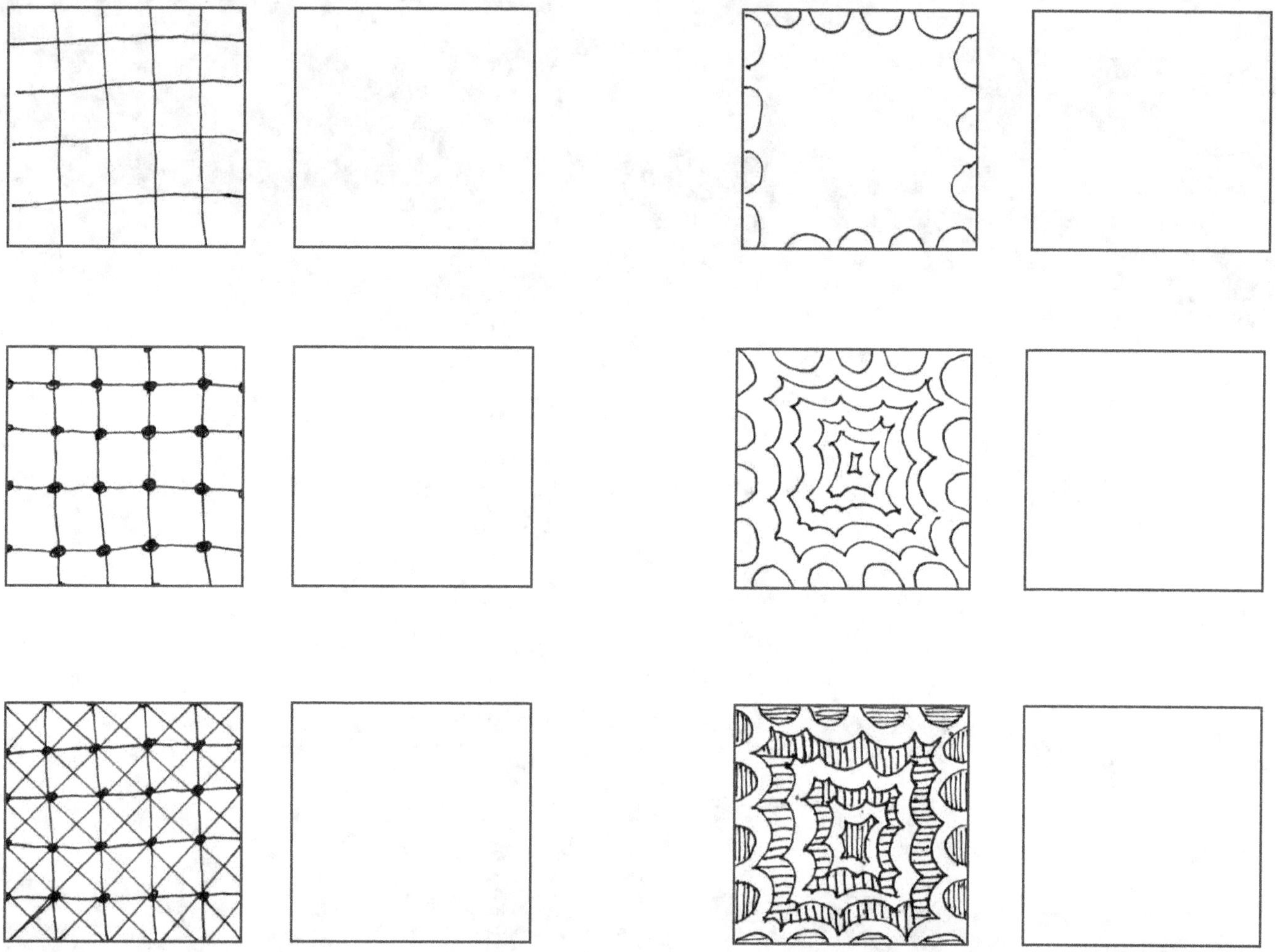

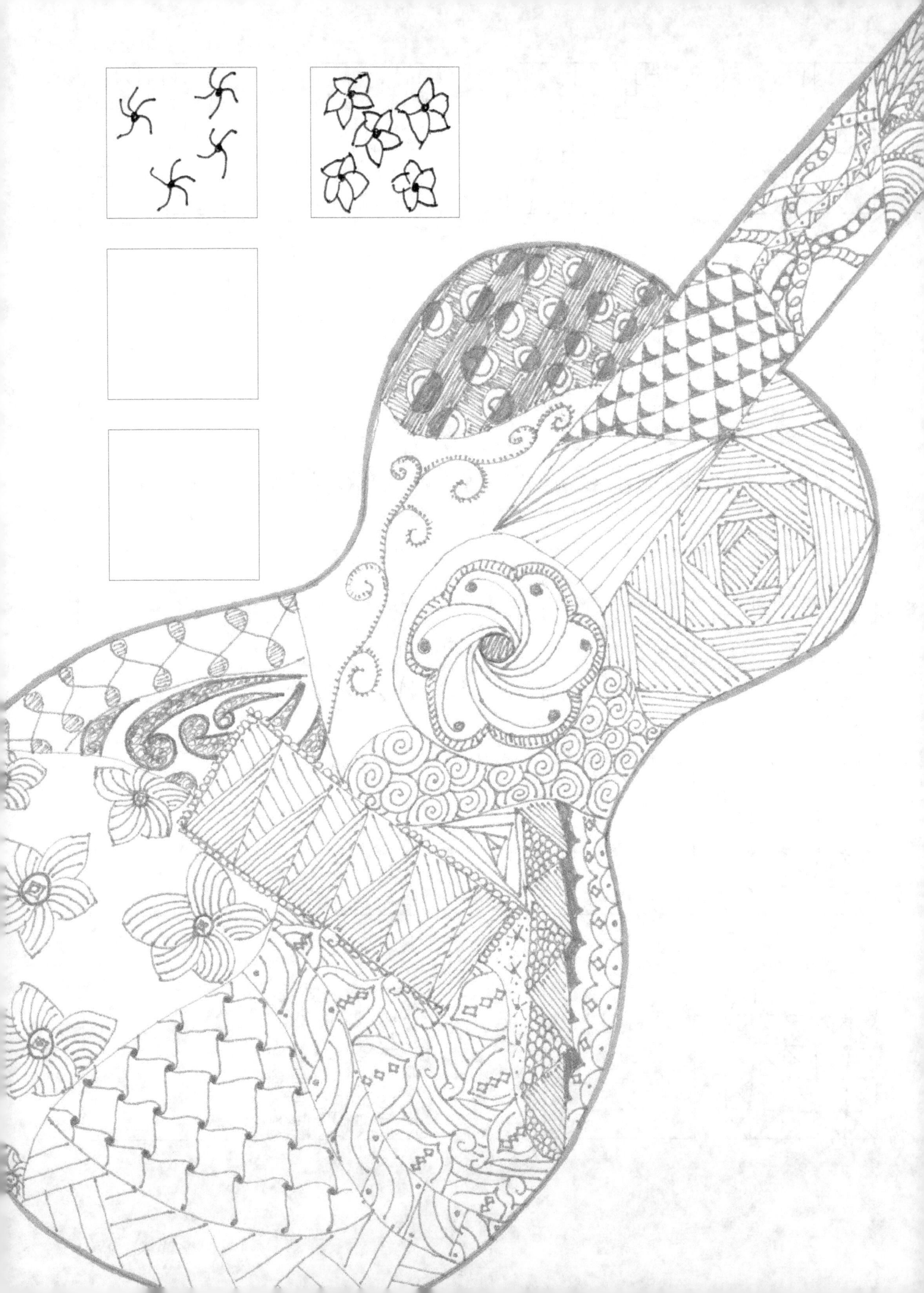

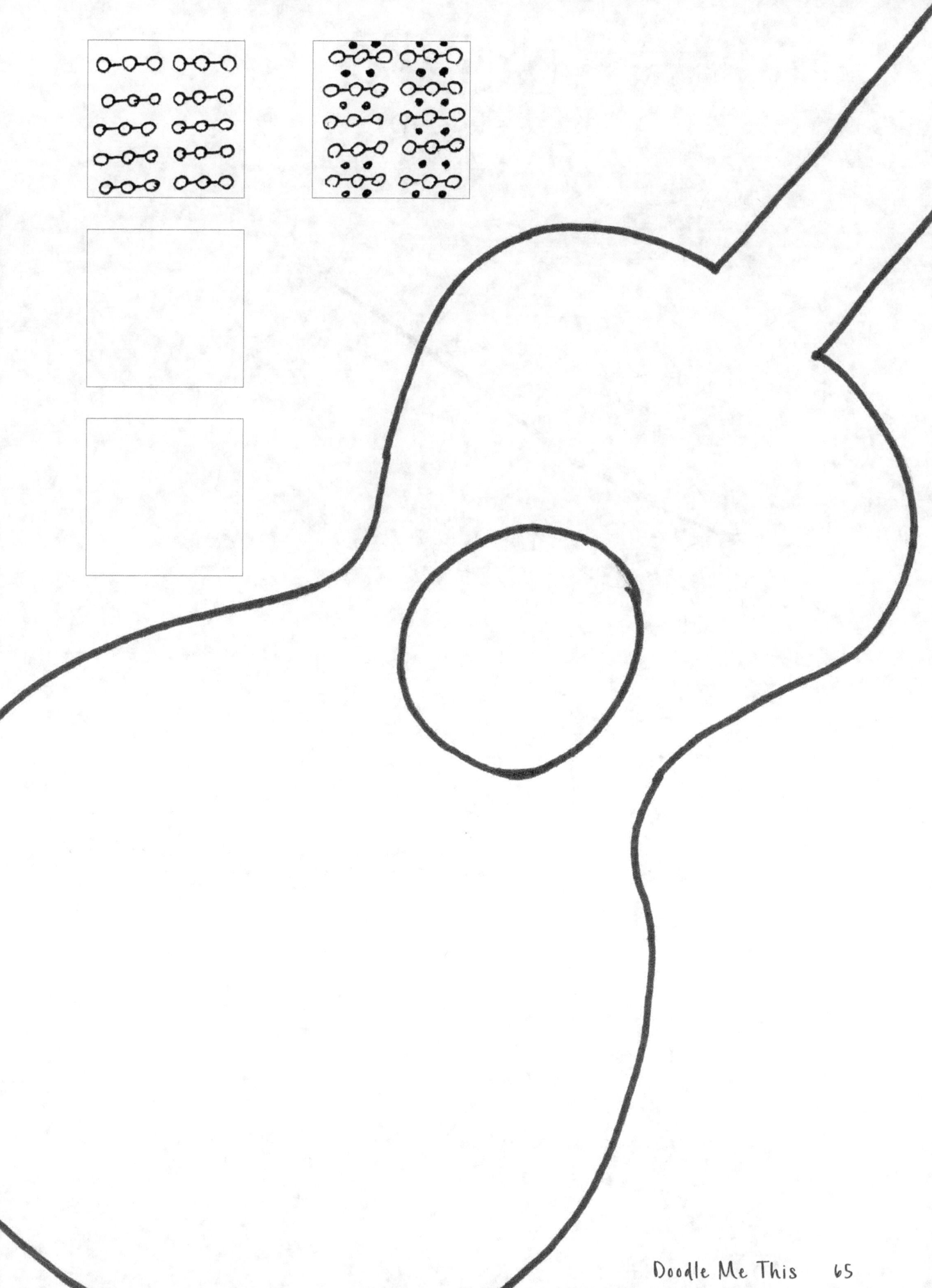

Nature

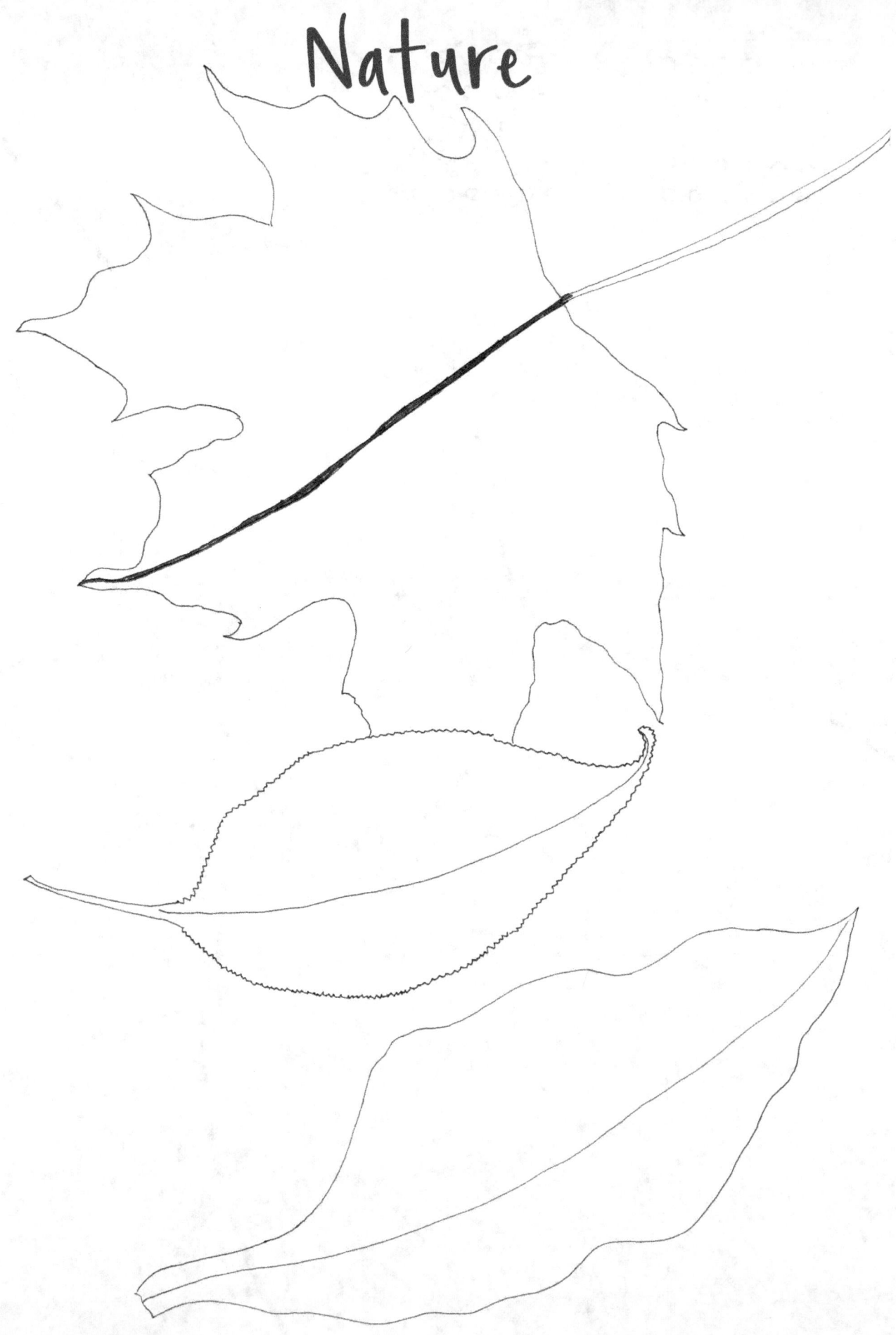

Doodle Me This

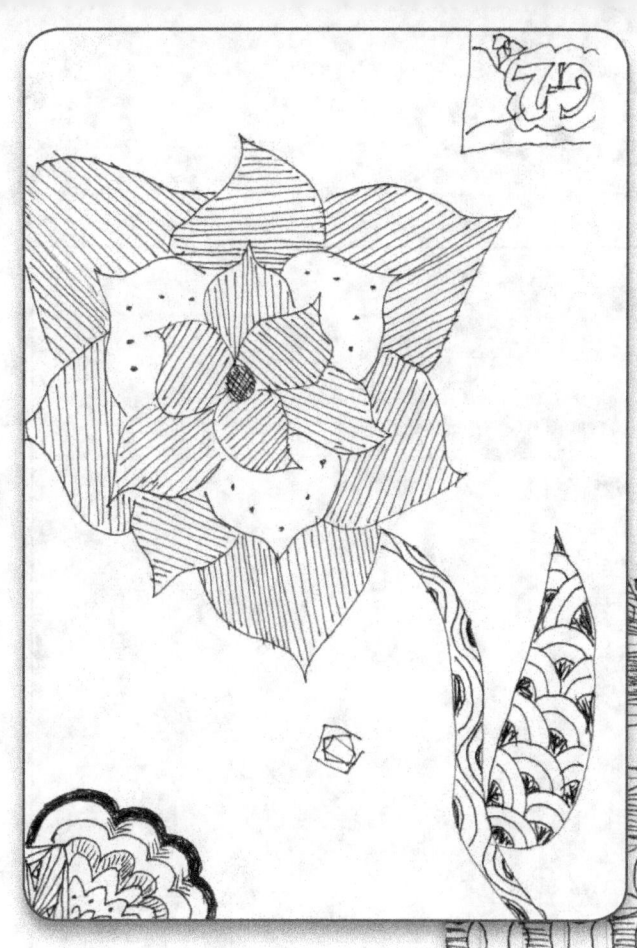

go outside.

Explore. Look at the trees, plants and flowers.

Grab some leaves or branches or both!

How about flowers, rocks, fossils, etc.? (you choose.)

Too bad you can't grab a rainbow...

As I write this, fall has just begun. The air is crisp and the leaves are amazing. Breathe in the air. Exhale. Are you ready to 🔺 ? Loosely trace your objects. Overlapping or separate.
Use COLORS!!!!

Possibilities are endless!

(that middle card in the background looks so straight and neat because I practiced on a lined notecard. I just added the verticals with a ruler. Then practiced the doodle - over and over. Try it!)

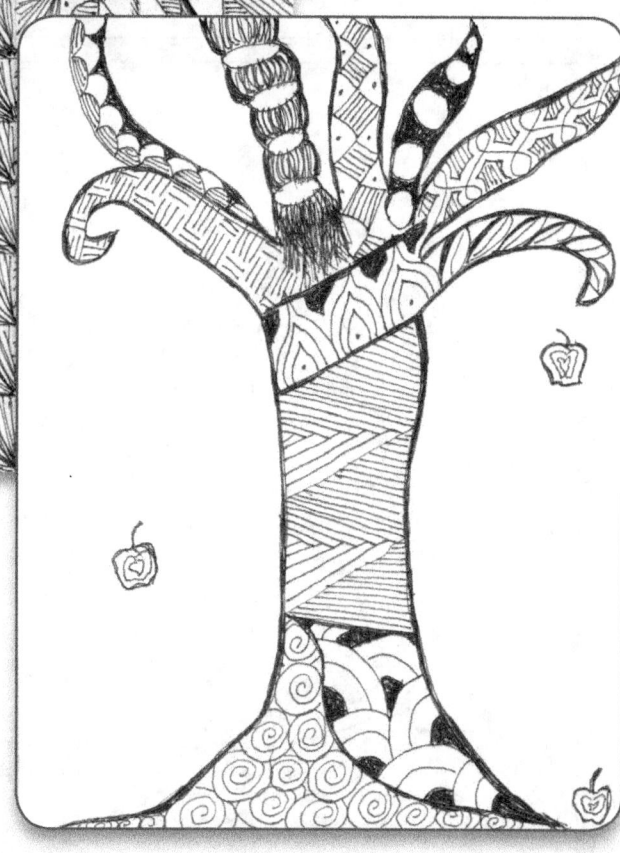

Name cards.

A friend sent me that card in the center on the right.

I have used it to make loads of cards for others...

I started with this outline.

Wrote the name. In pencil first, of course.

Then separated the rest of the page and used

different doodles in each section.

Use ideas from what you see.

Remember patterns are EVERYWHERE!

You can use others' ideas to create your own style

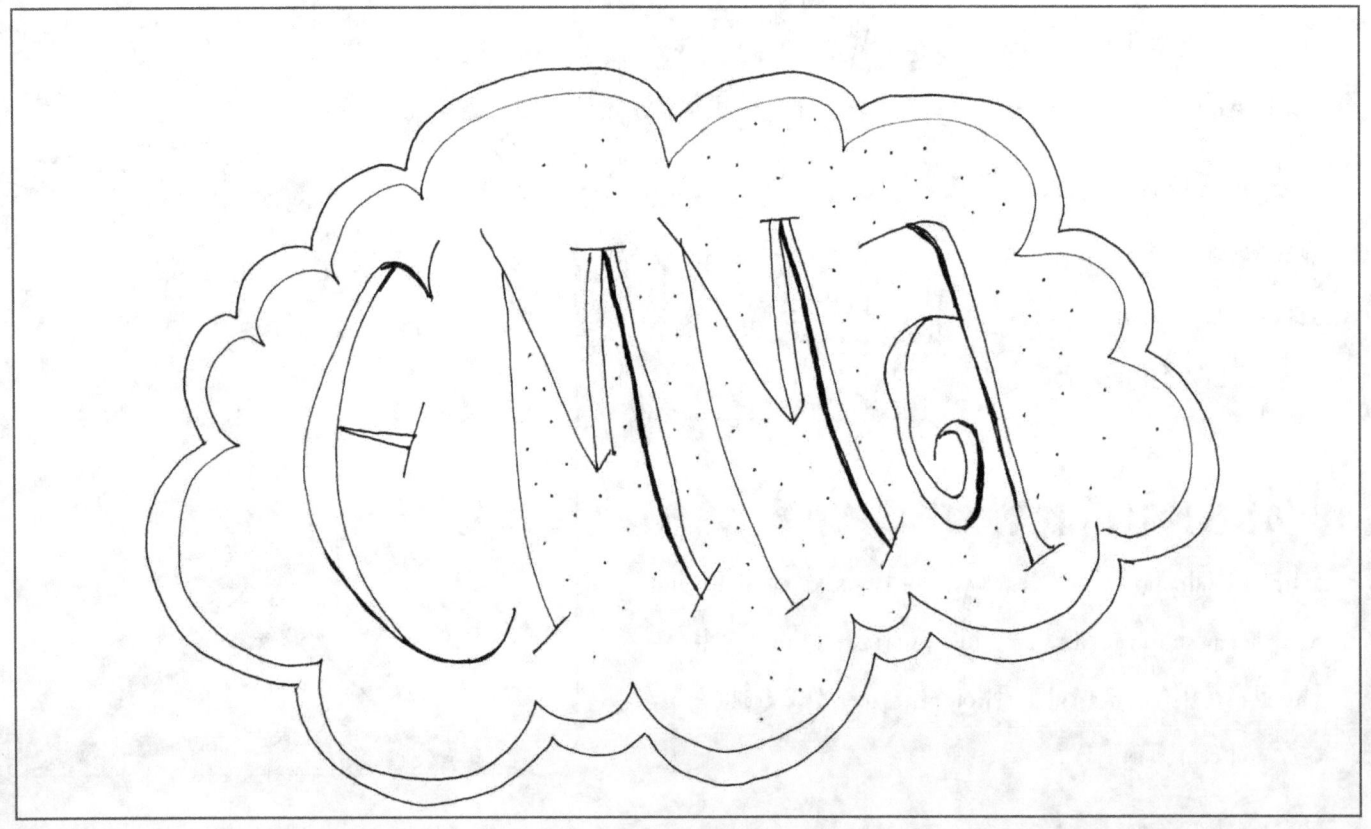

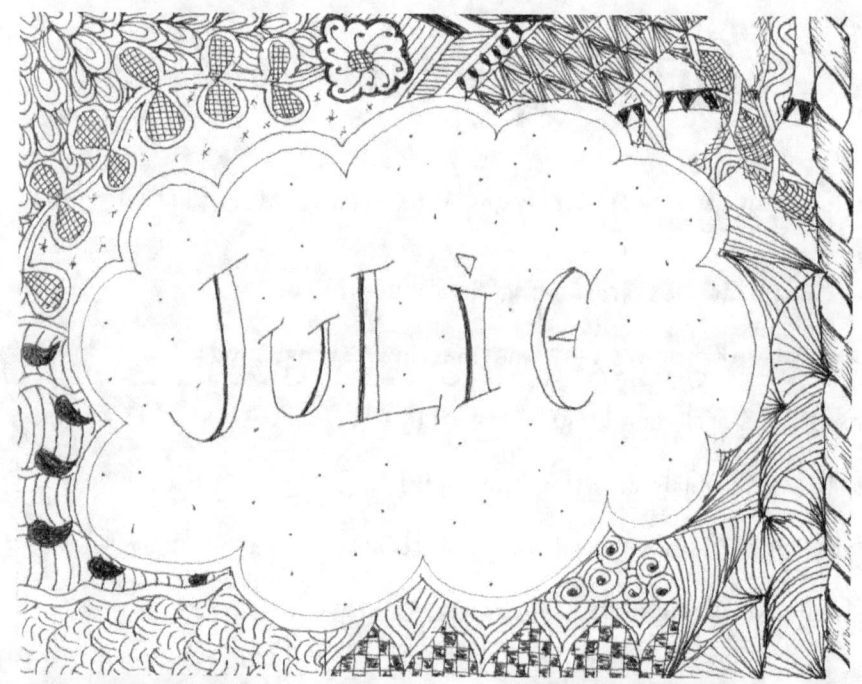

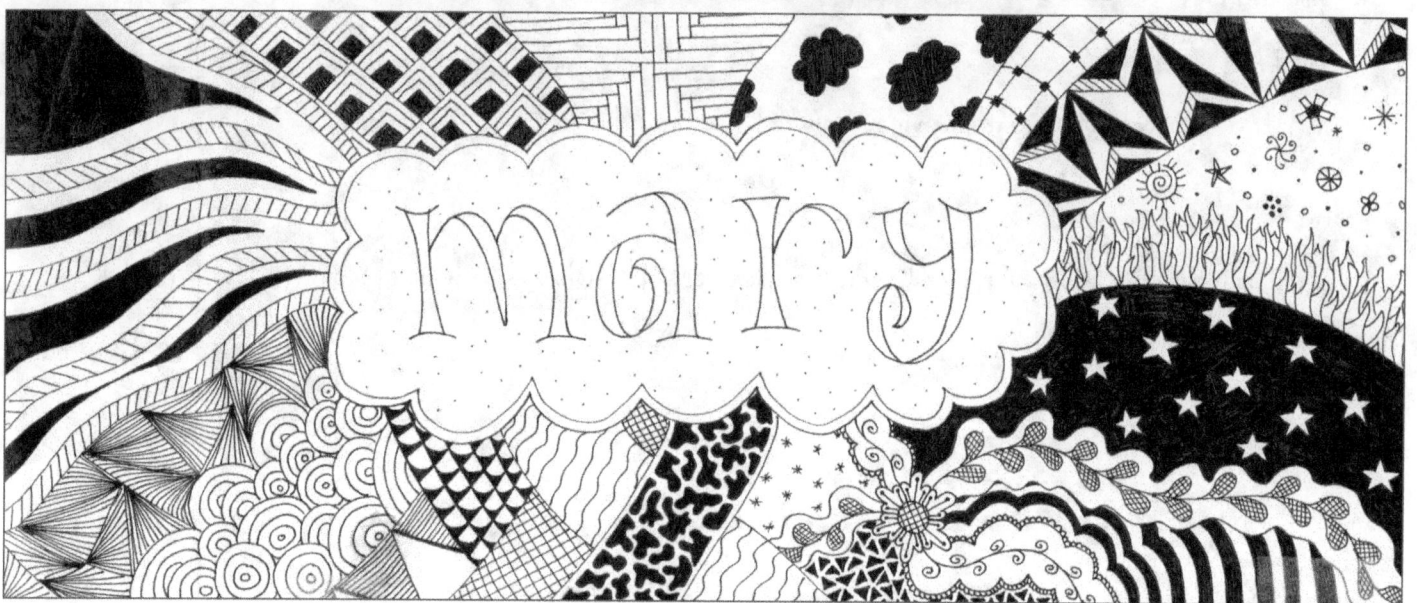

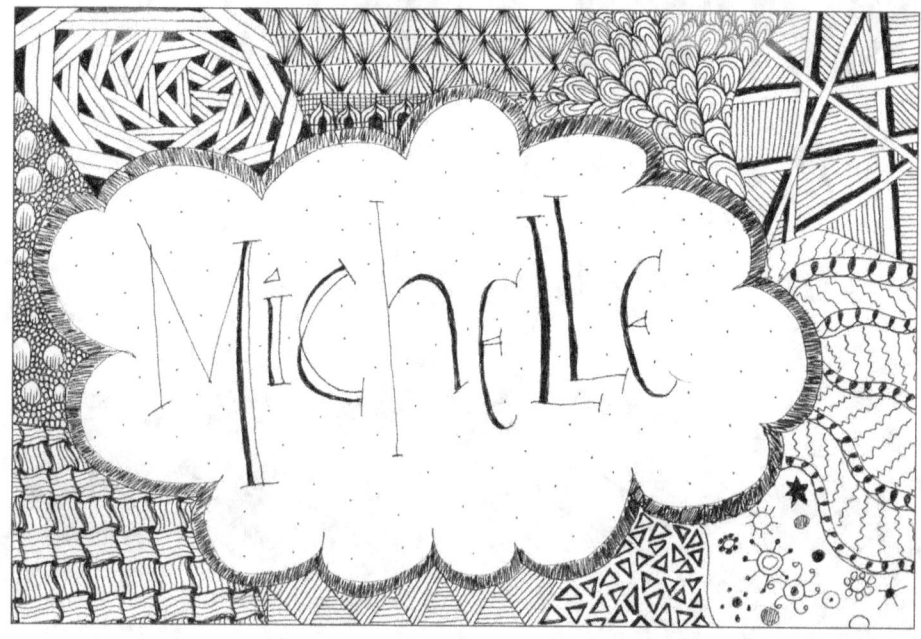

Gifting Your Doodles.

You might not believe your 🔺 are worth anything... read postcard below!

What do you do with your doodles, drawings and colorings?

If you are doodling and think you are just wasting time - maybe not!

Many of the ideas in this book can be used for gifts.

Keep all those doodles on hand to create gifts of all kinds:

~ Cards, letters, postcards. Send by snail mail... Birthday, Sympathy, Hello, Thank You, I'm Sorry and "You just may be my best friend in the whole world right now" cards.

~ Bookmarks

~ Wall Art

~ Tattoos(?) What? It's been known to happen!

Hint:

Put all your doodles in one place and each month check for holidays, b-days, etc. - have them ready!

Who doesn't love a handmade gift?

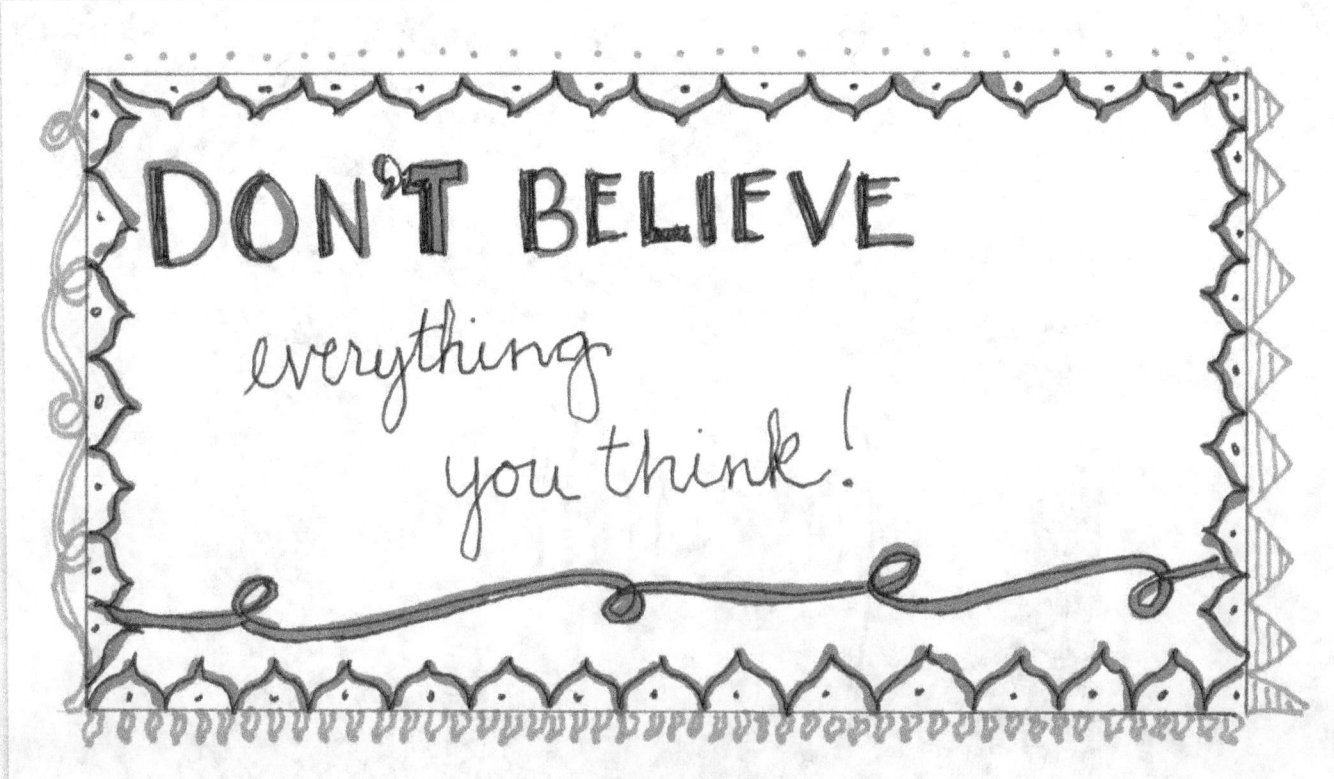

DON'T BELIEVE
everything
you think!

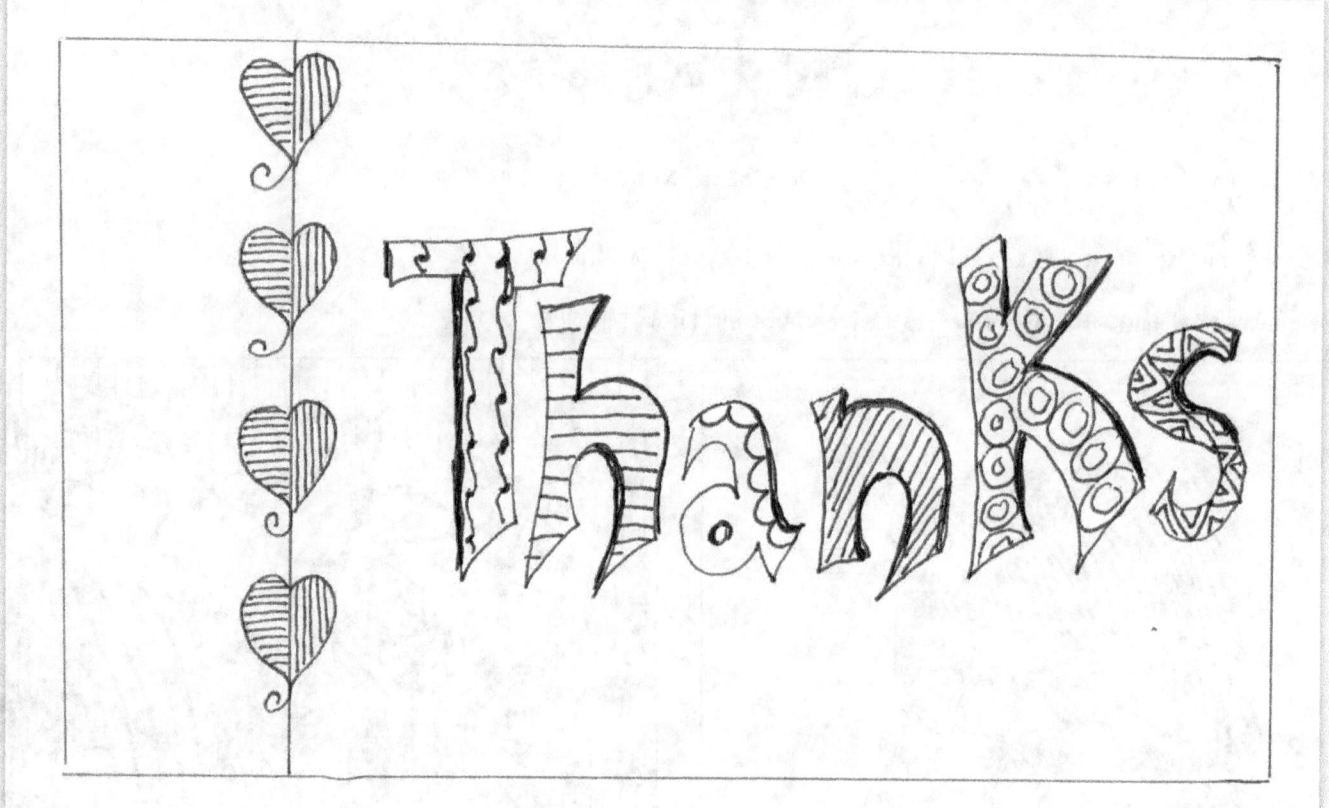

I LOVE to go to people's houses and find these cards and doodles on their fridge, from YEARS ago. That feels pretty good. You know why? I say to myself,, "Wow, I did that?"

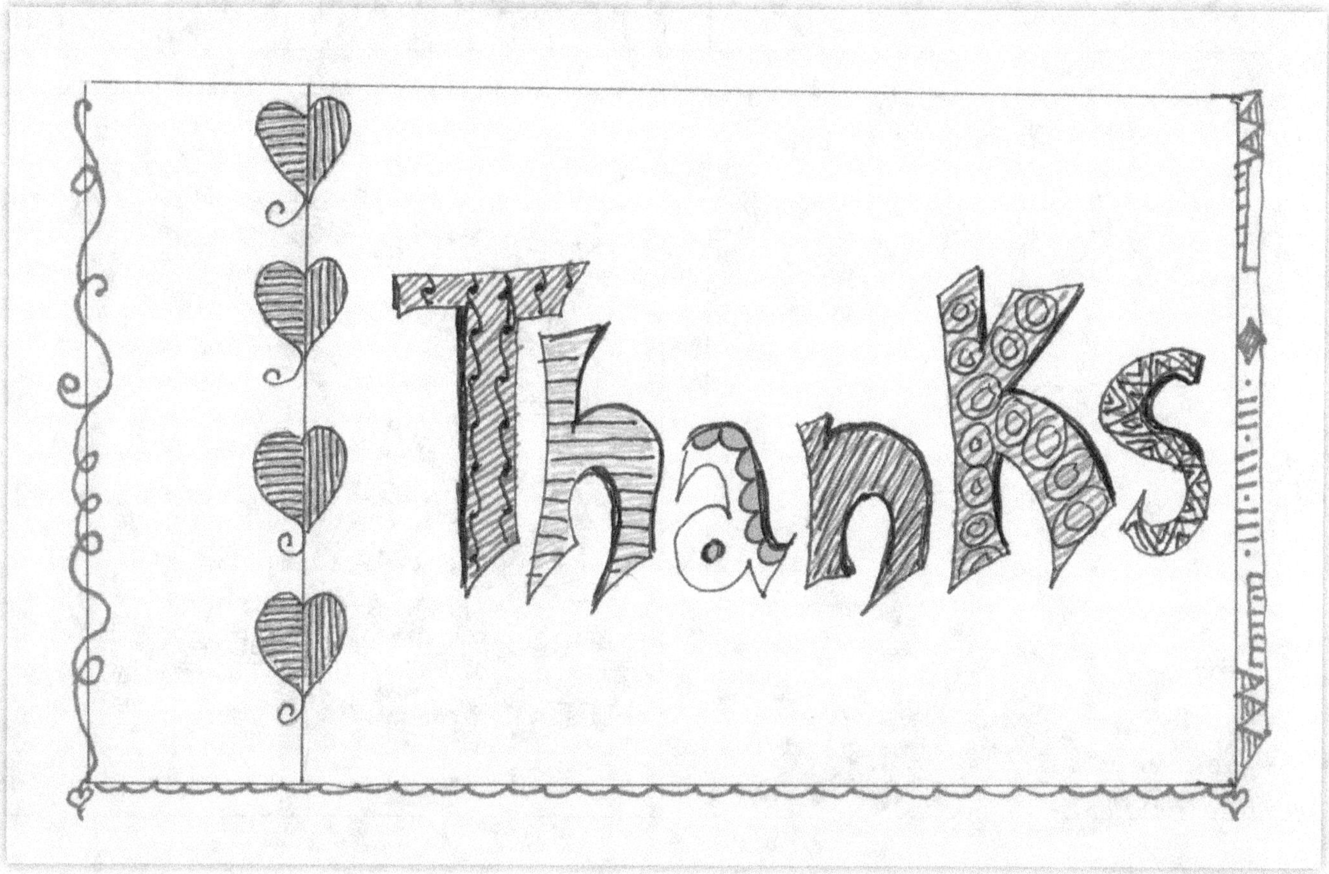

On the go.

I just carry these 4 X 4 cards that I got on Amazon everywhere I go.

When I feel the need to , I pull one out and start doodling!

You can make your own by using card stock and cutting it in 1/4s.

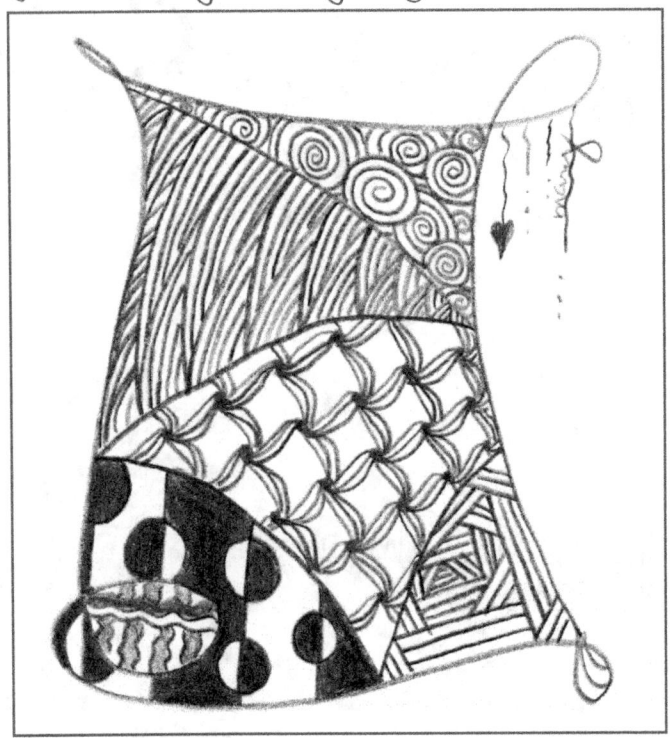
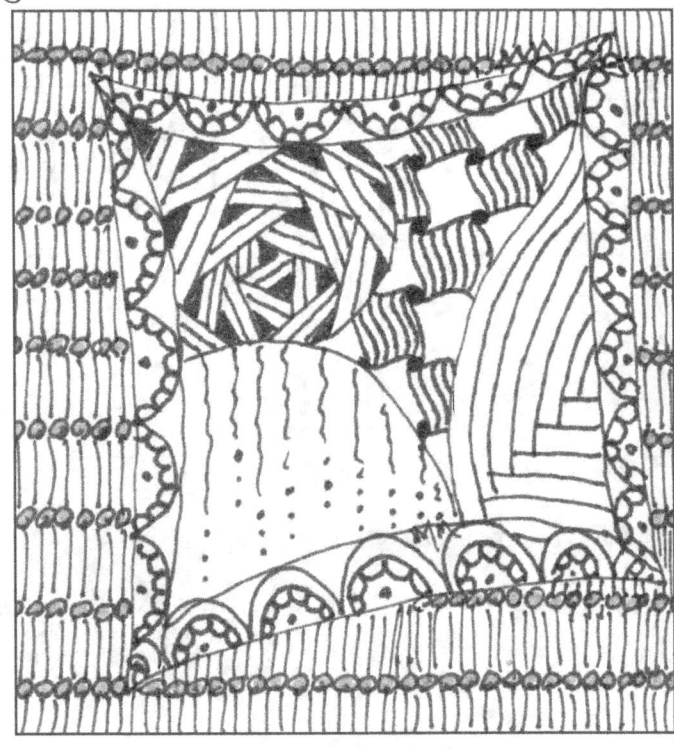
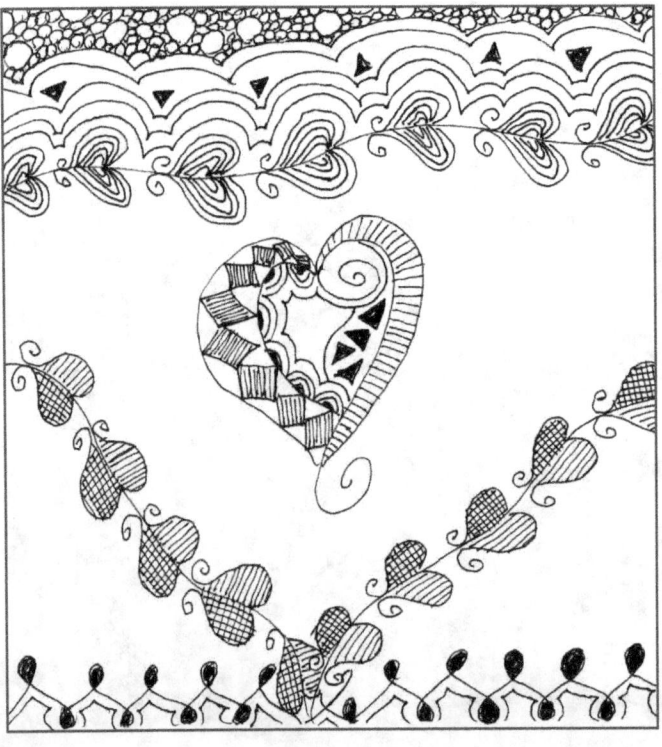
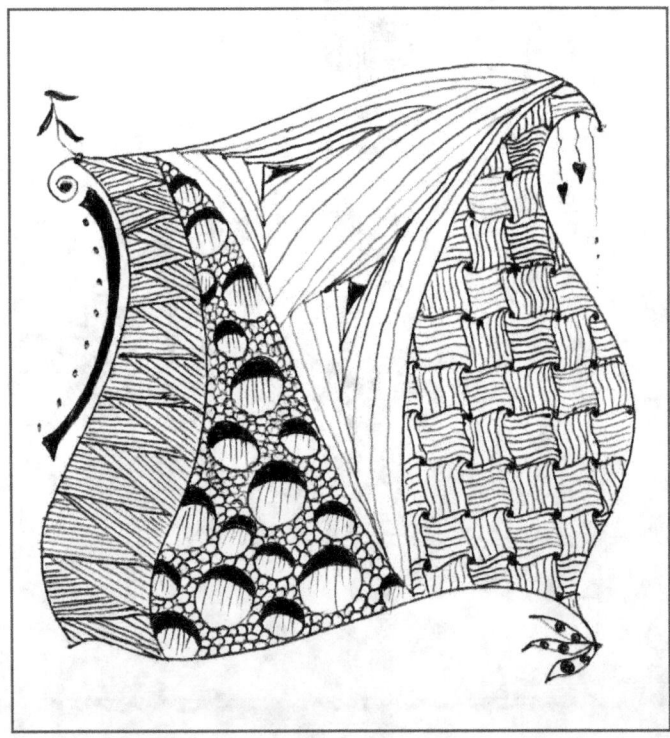

Bookmarks.

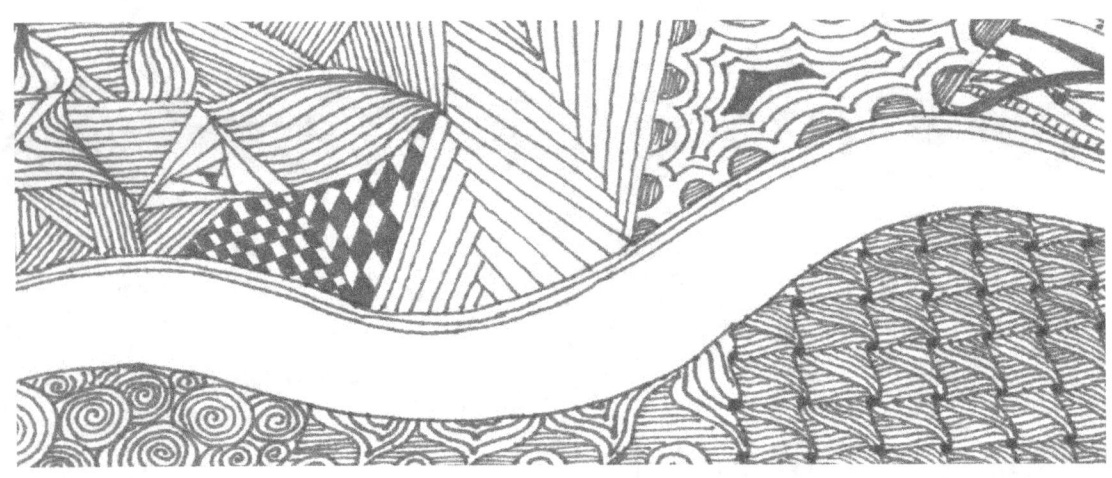

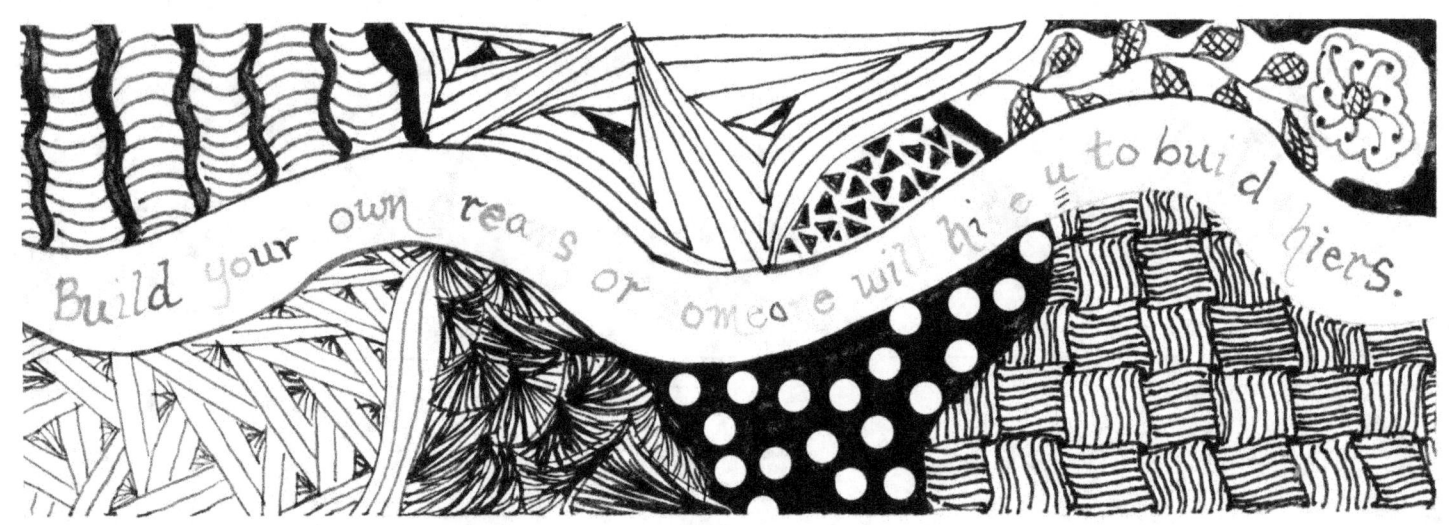

Build your own reams or omeoe will hire u to build hiers.

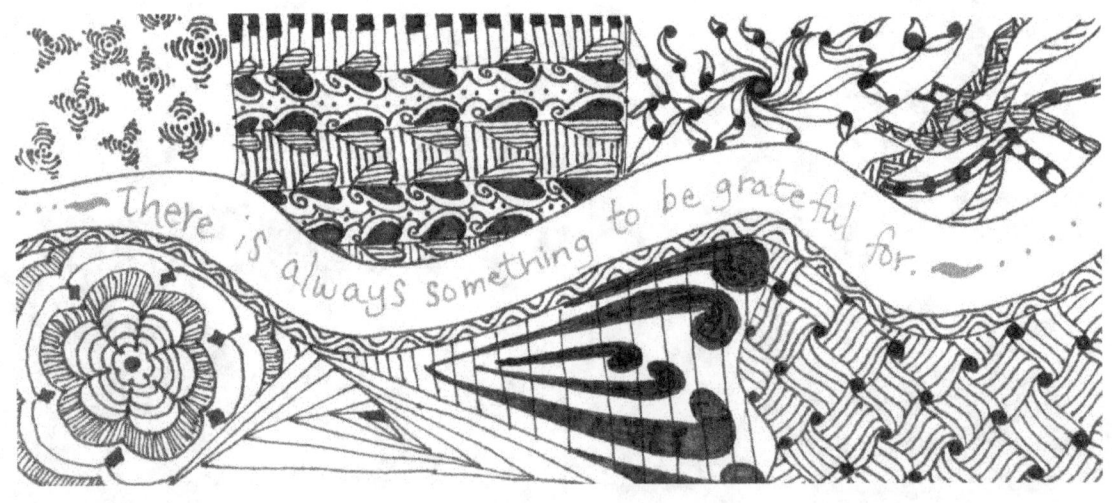

....—there is always something to be grateful for.—.....

Yep. I do know there is a miskate on this page. Can you find it? Email me...

This 8.5x11 piece of card stock makes 4 bookmarks perfectly!

Remember more templates are in the back so go ahead and doodle on these.

More bookmarks, ornaments, Christmas cards ideas!

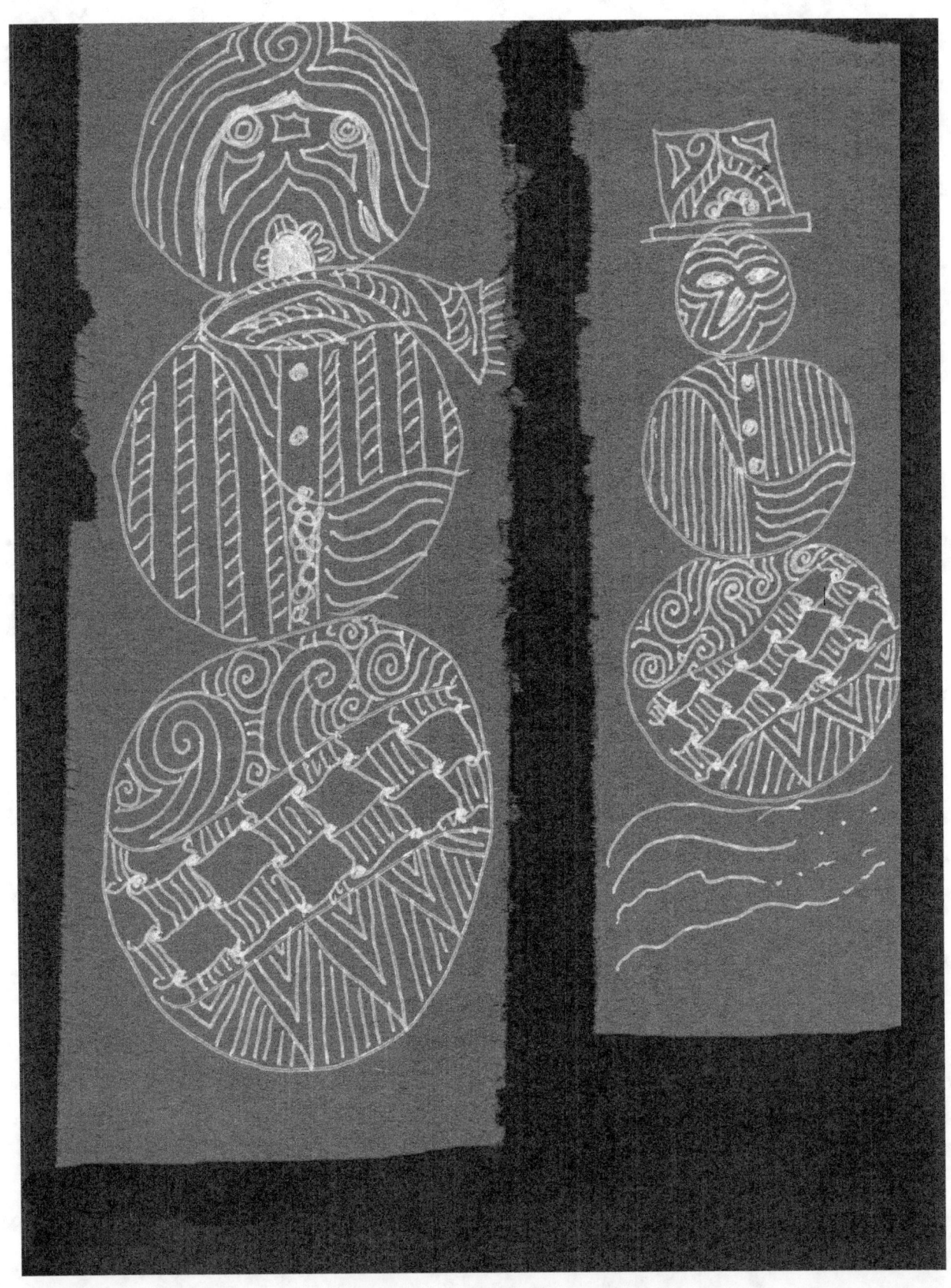

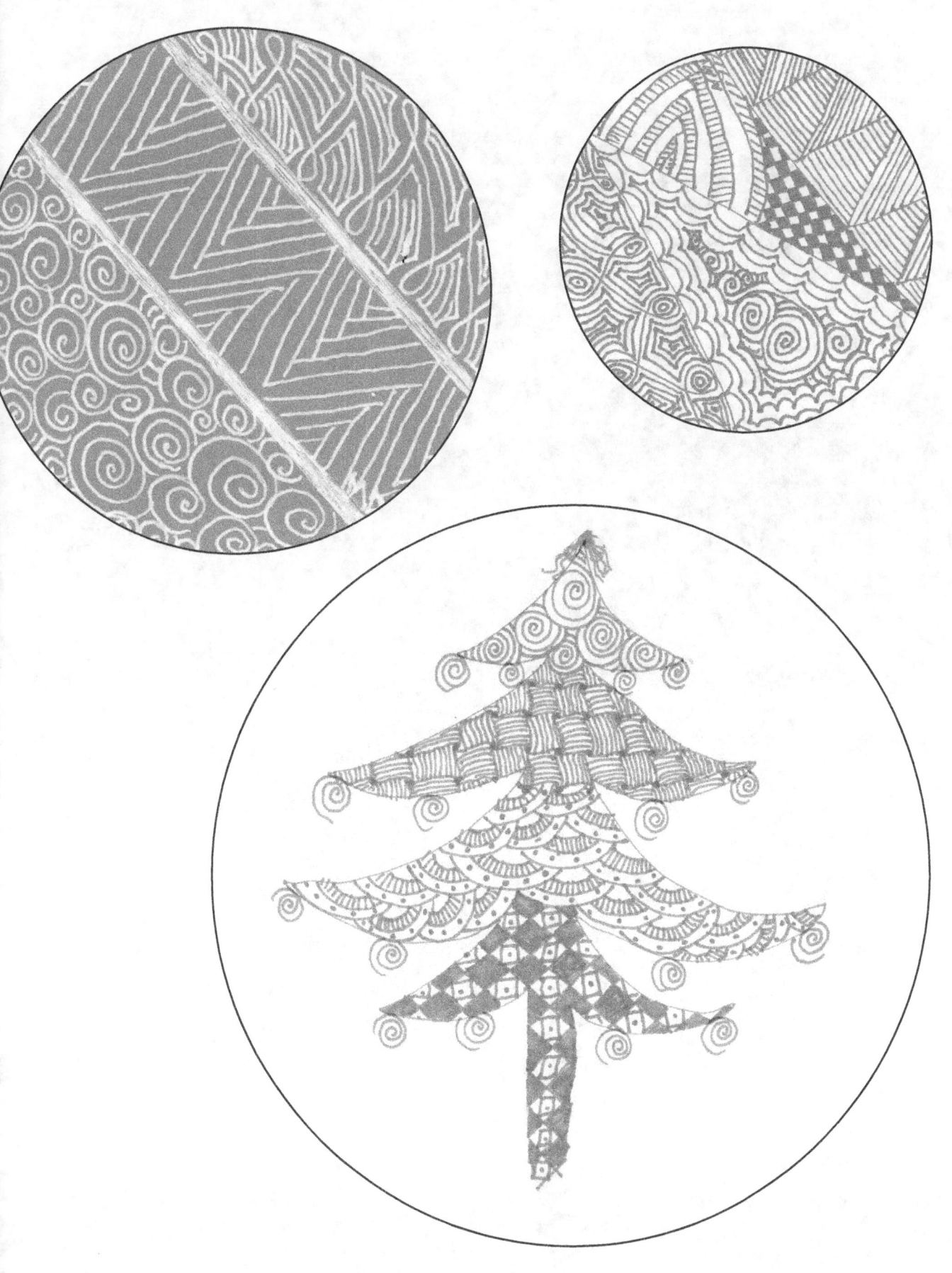

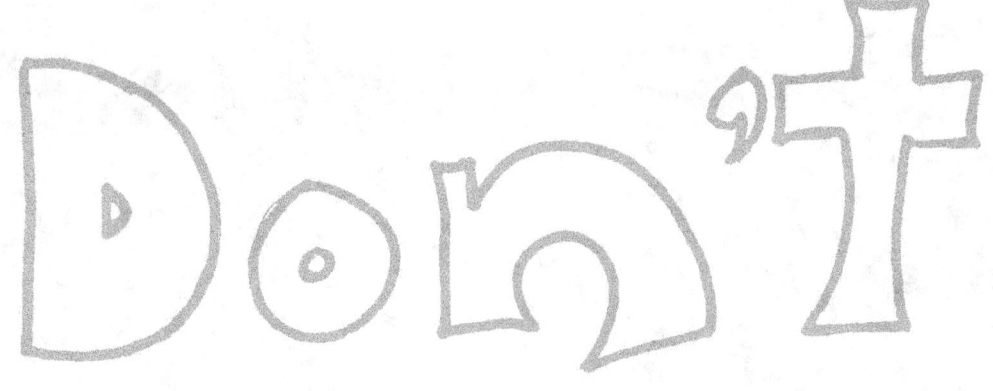

Don't You Worry.

(Doodle in these letters with your favorite patterns)

Doodle Me This

The way to draw well, is to draw!

 helps quiet your soul and awaken your curiosity.

Set a timer, start with two minutes.

Yes, two minutes.

Two minutes is do-able.

A few things can happen:

1. You will start to notice your mind and body relax. (You really will.)

2. Eventually more than two minutes will pass. As you get better, you can set the timer for three minutes, yes, three minutes! And so on and so forth...

3. You have now started a habit that can become a two-minute (or more) mental health "break".

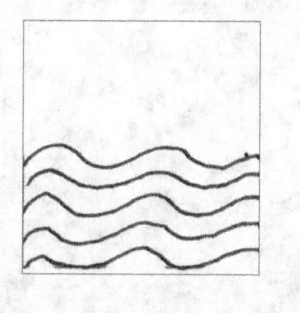

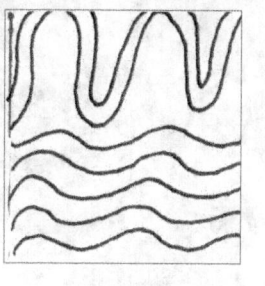

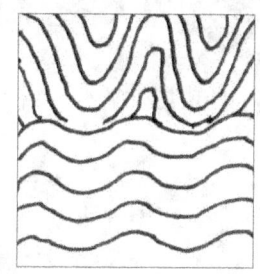

Don't you worry if:

~you're not doing it perfectly

~you don't like what you've done

~you feel you are wasting time

~ you're thinking, " There is SO MUCH ELSE I SHOULD BE DOING!"

Just try it. Who knows?

No one died doodling for two minutes. No reported cases anyway.   ;)

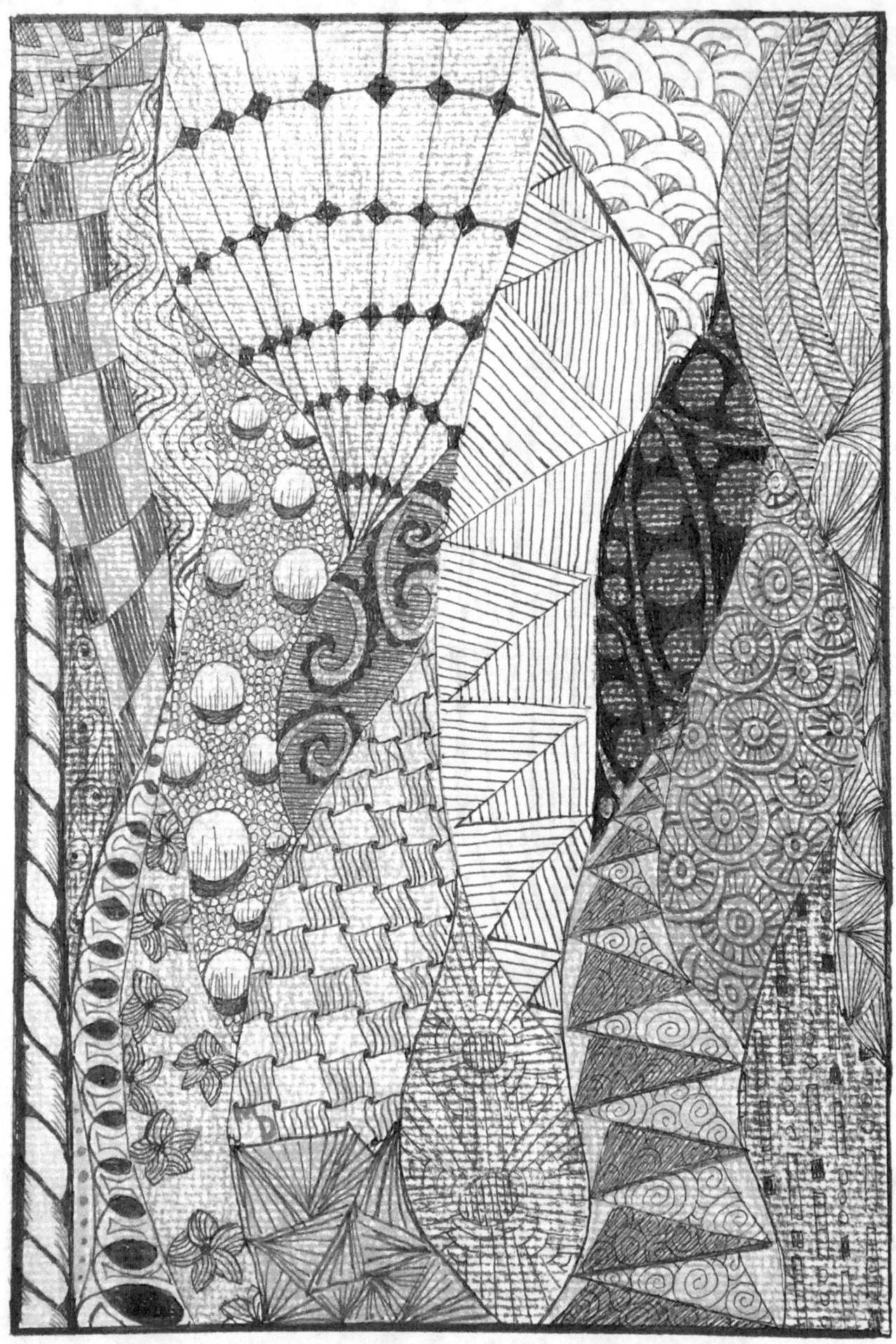

Doodle Me This

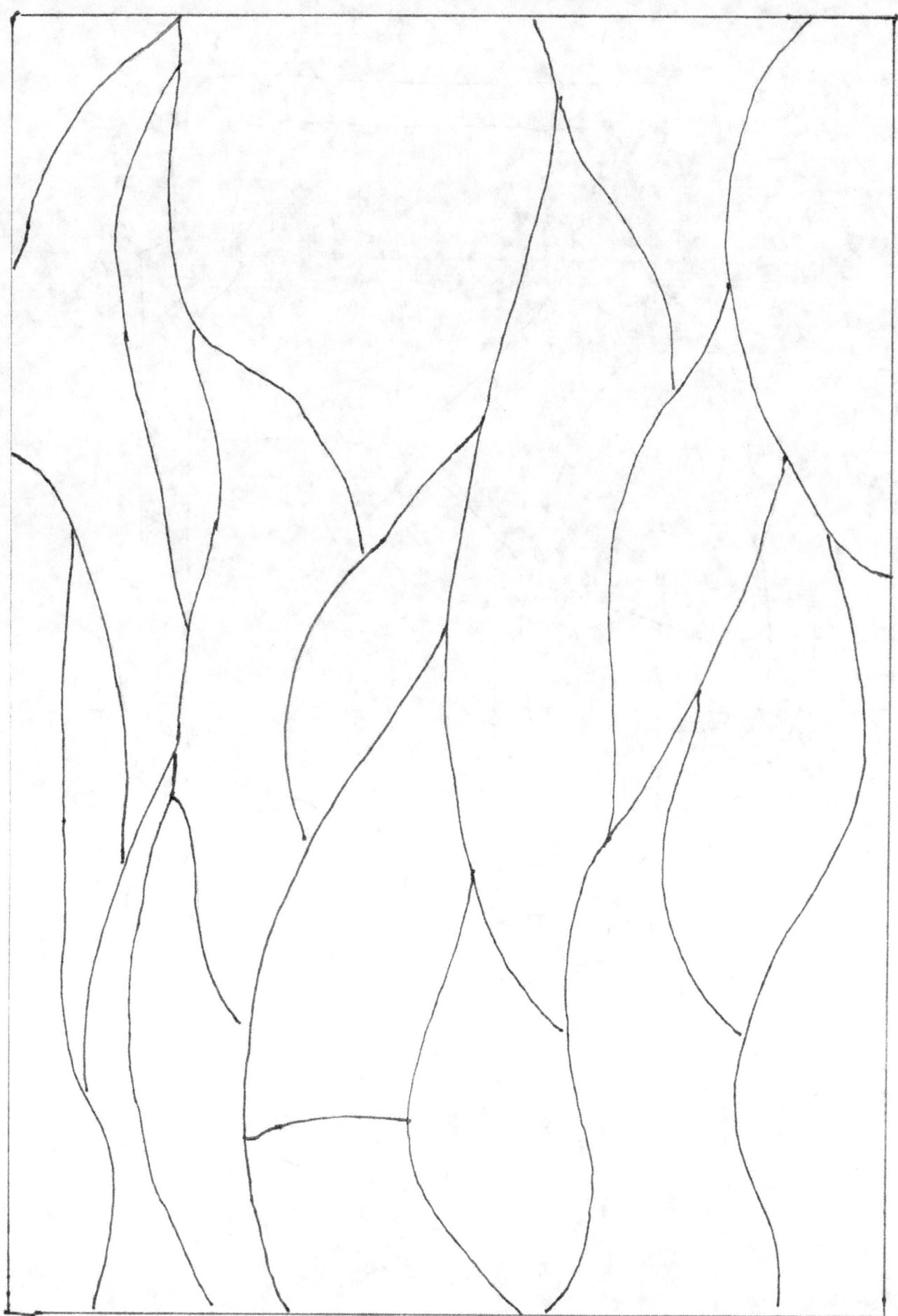

Billy, thanks for always taking my 'emergency' PS calls.

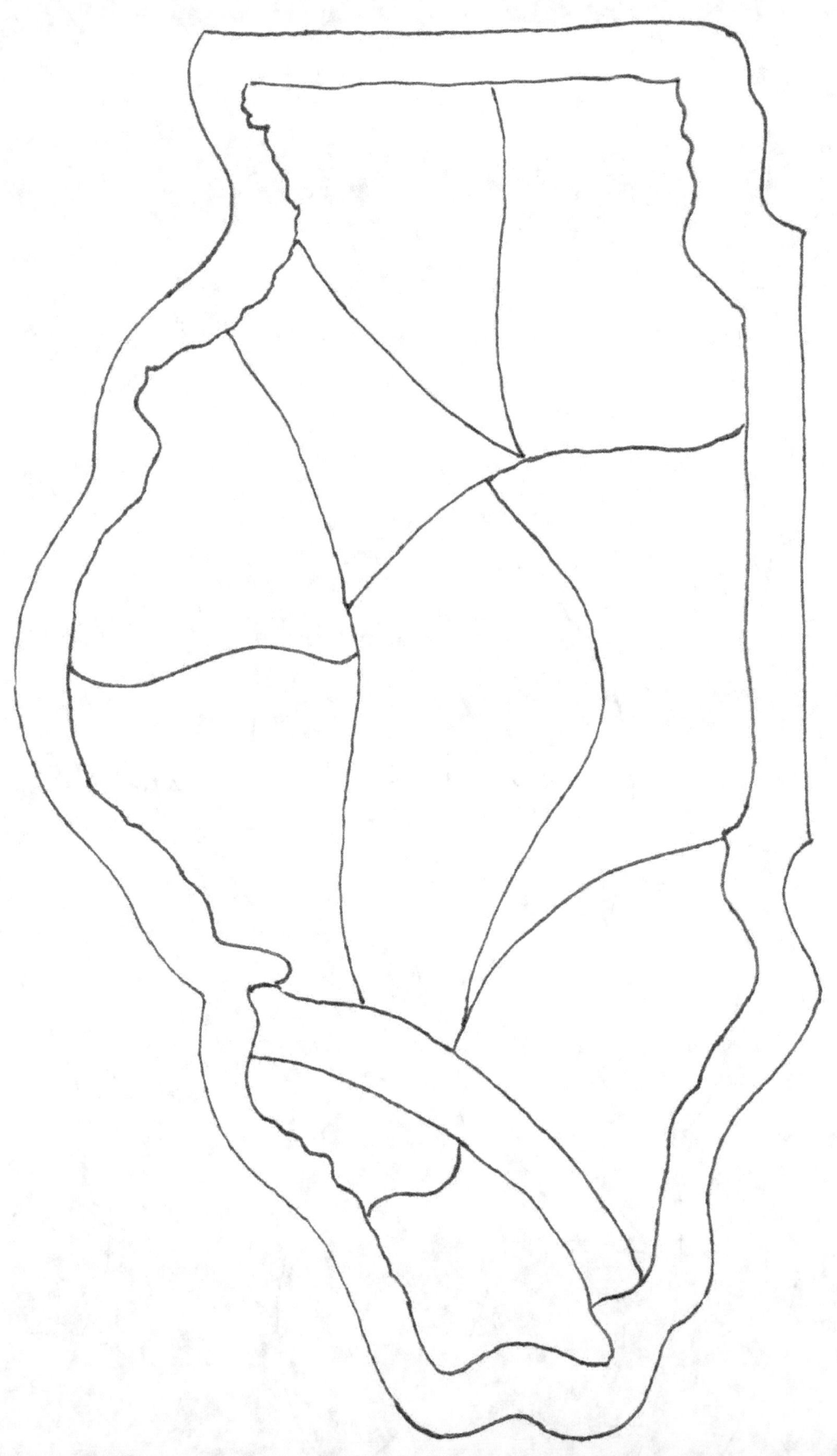

Doodle Me This

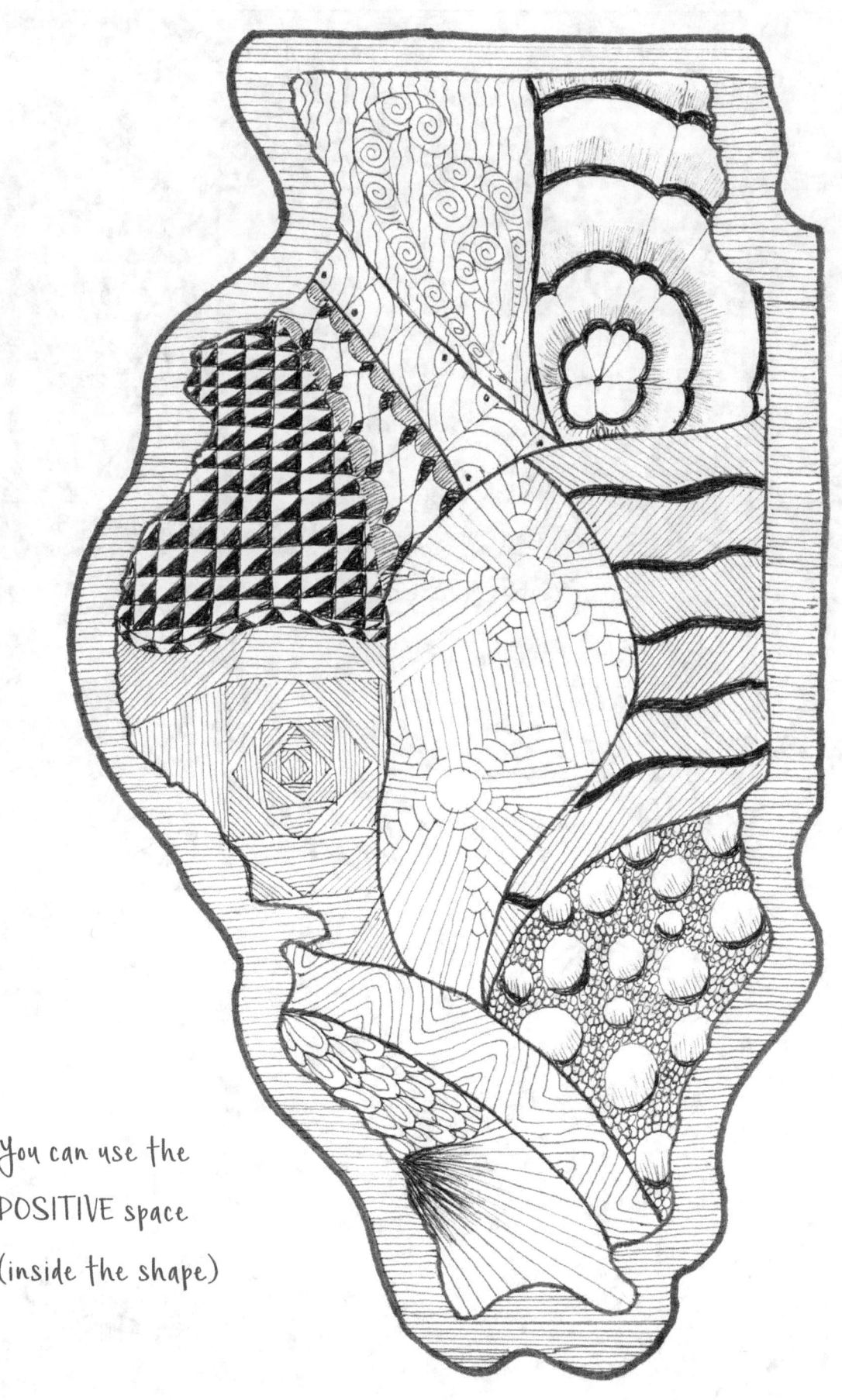

You can use the
POSITIVE space
(inside the shape)

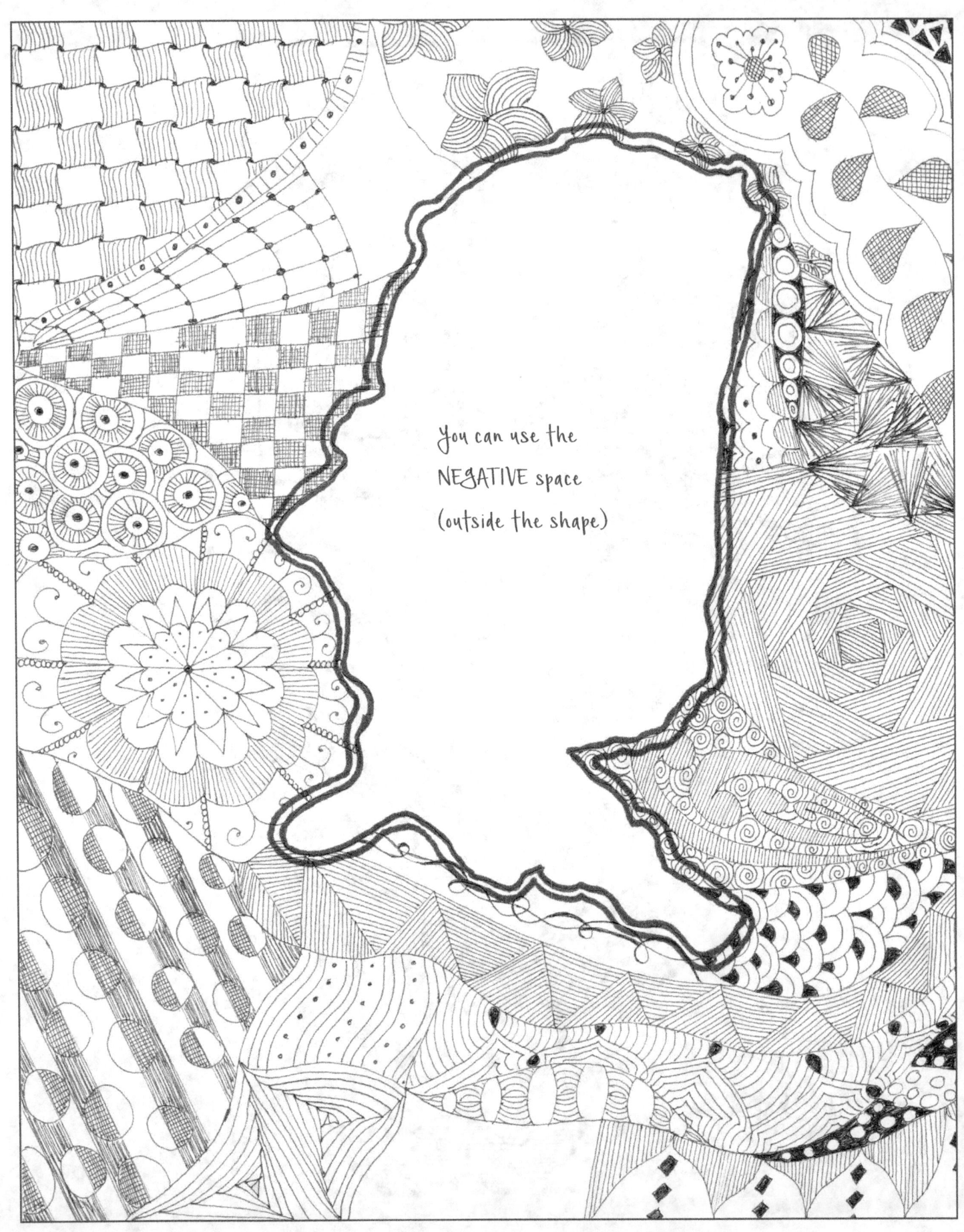

You can use the
NEGATIVE space
(outside the shape)

Doodle Me This

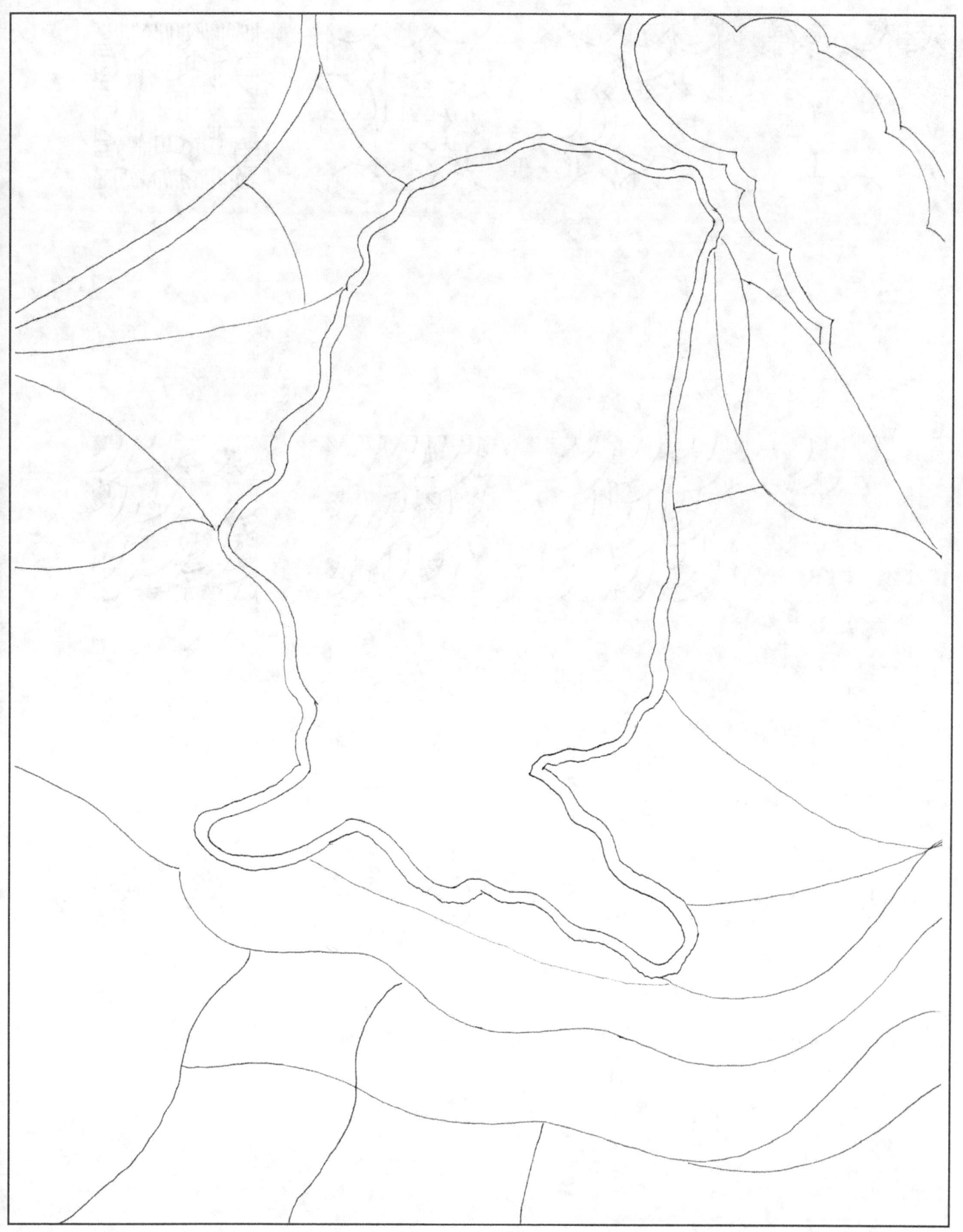

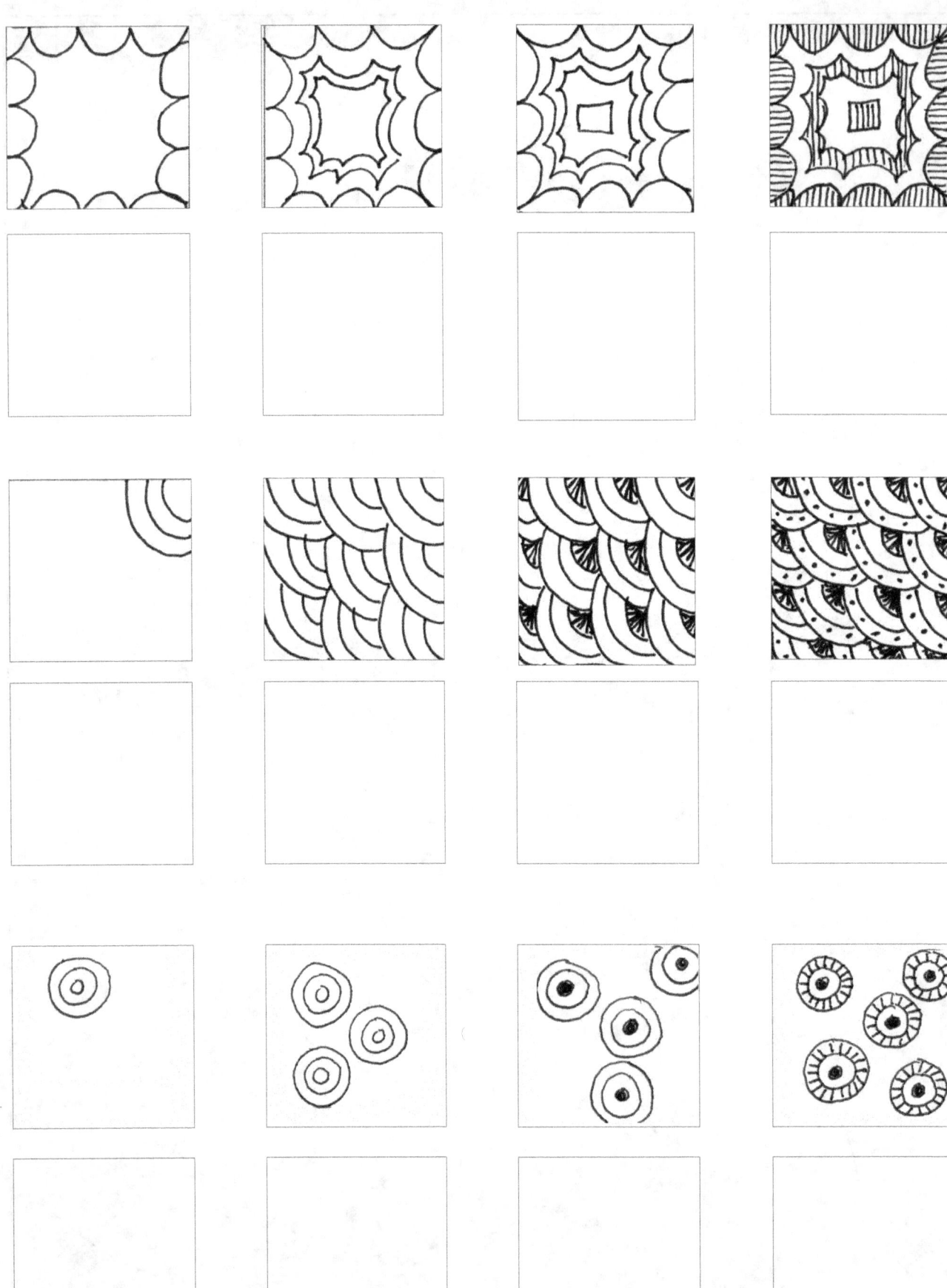

Doodle Me This

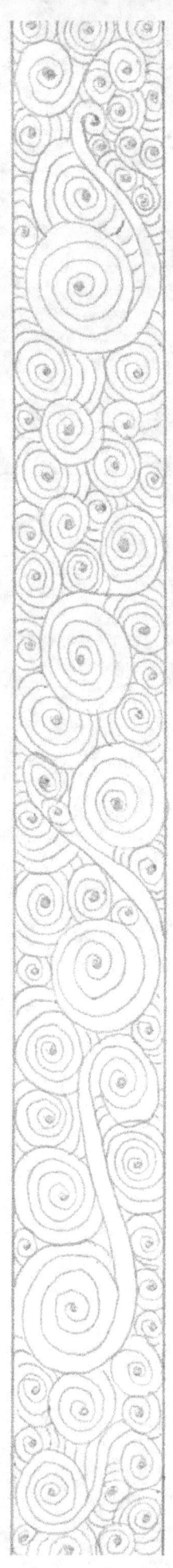

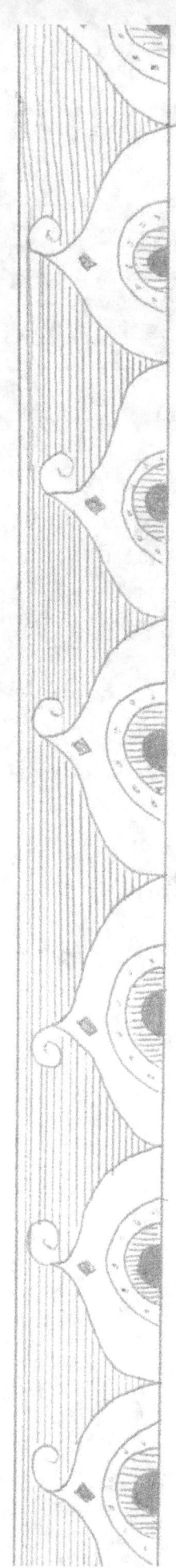

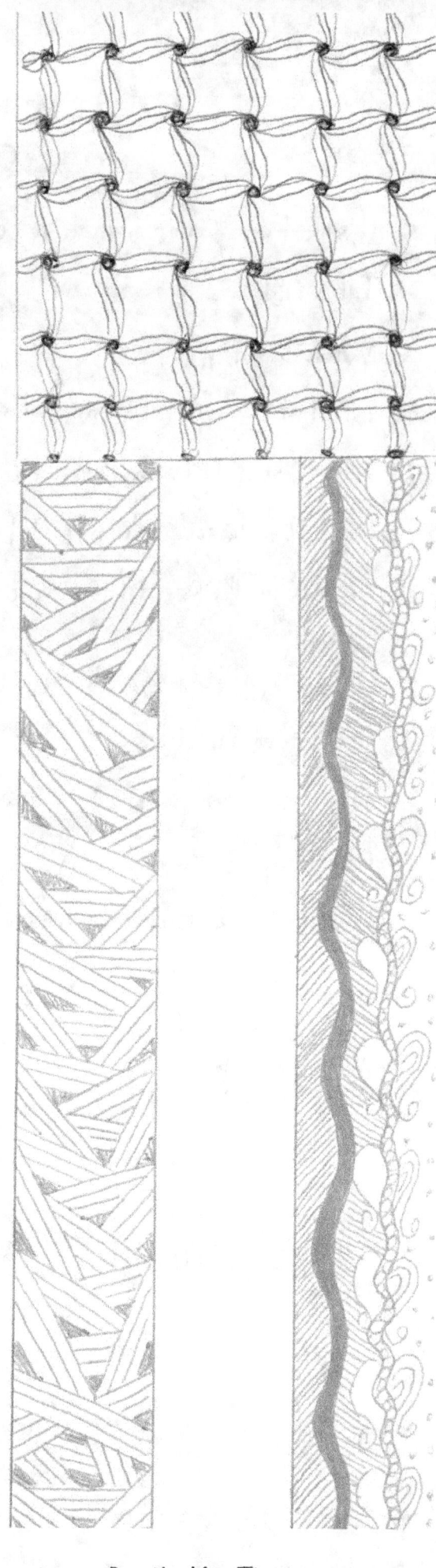

Follow your curiosity.

It's just △, not a whole lot can go wrong.

Take risks.

Make stuff up.

What if I draw this? And then add this?

What about this line with that squiggle?

Does it look good? Keep it. Not so good? Erase it.

This is just PRACTiCE. Smile and laugh once in a while.

Observe patterns in the world.

Use them for ideas.

(They are everywhere.)

One night while watching "Call The Midwife" on PBS,

I noticed a pattern on a dress that I thought would make a perfect doodle.

Here is my version... ⇨ ⇨ ⇨ ⇨ ⇨ ⇨ ⇨

Awesome, right?

Look around right now and find a pattern. Draw it!

What makes you happy when you △ on the pages? Do that.

Have fun!

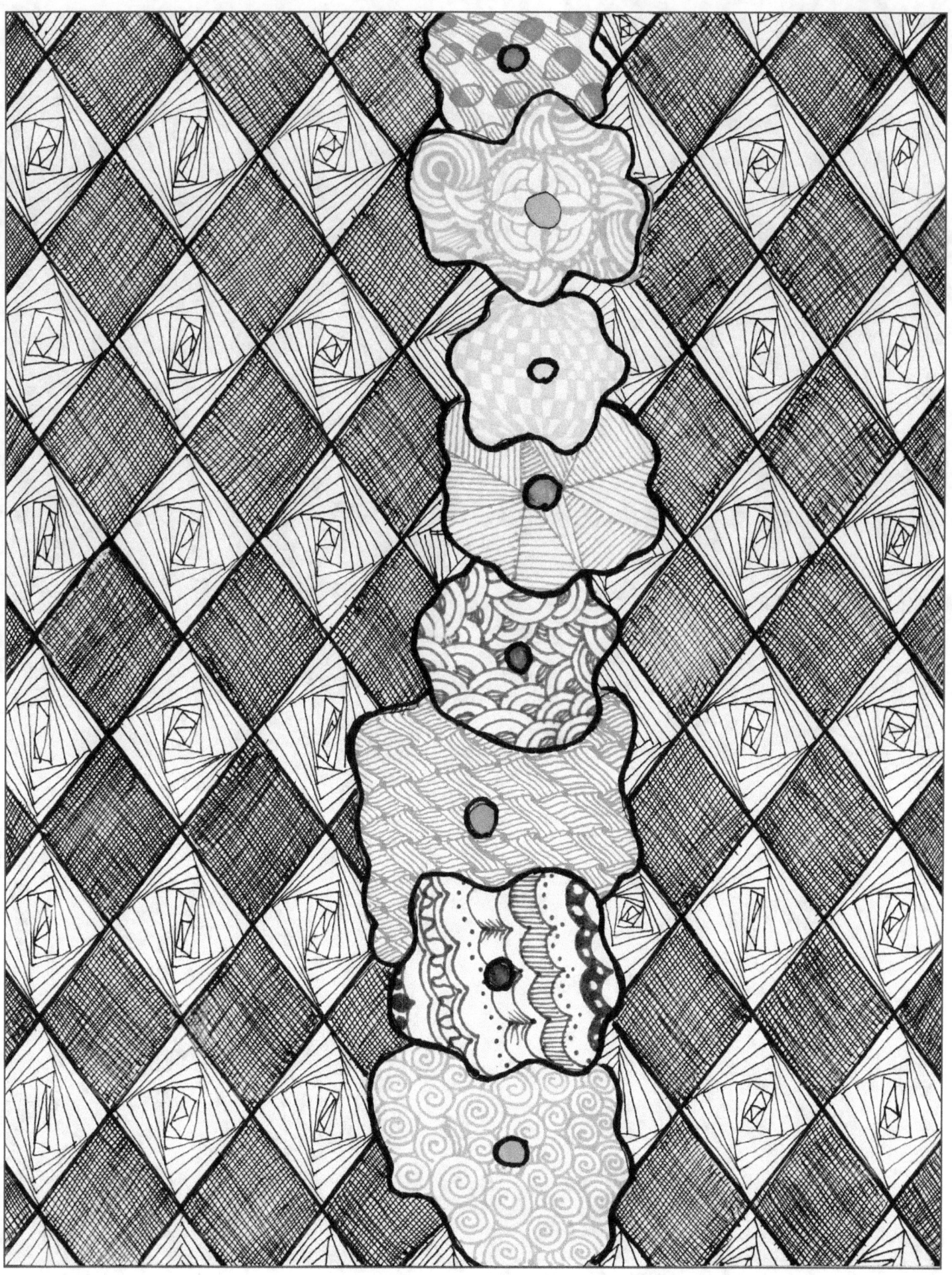

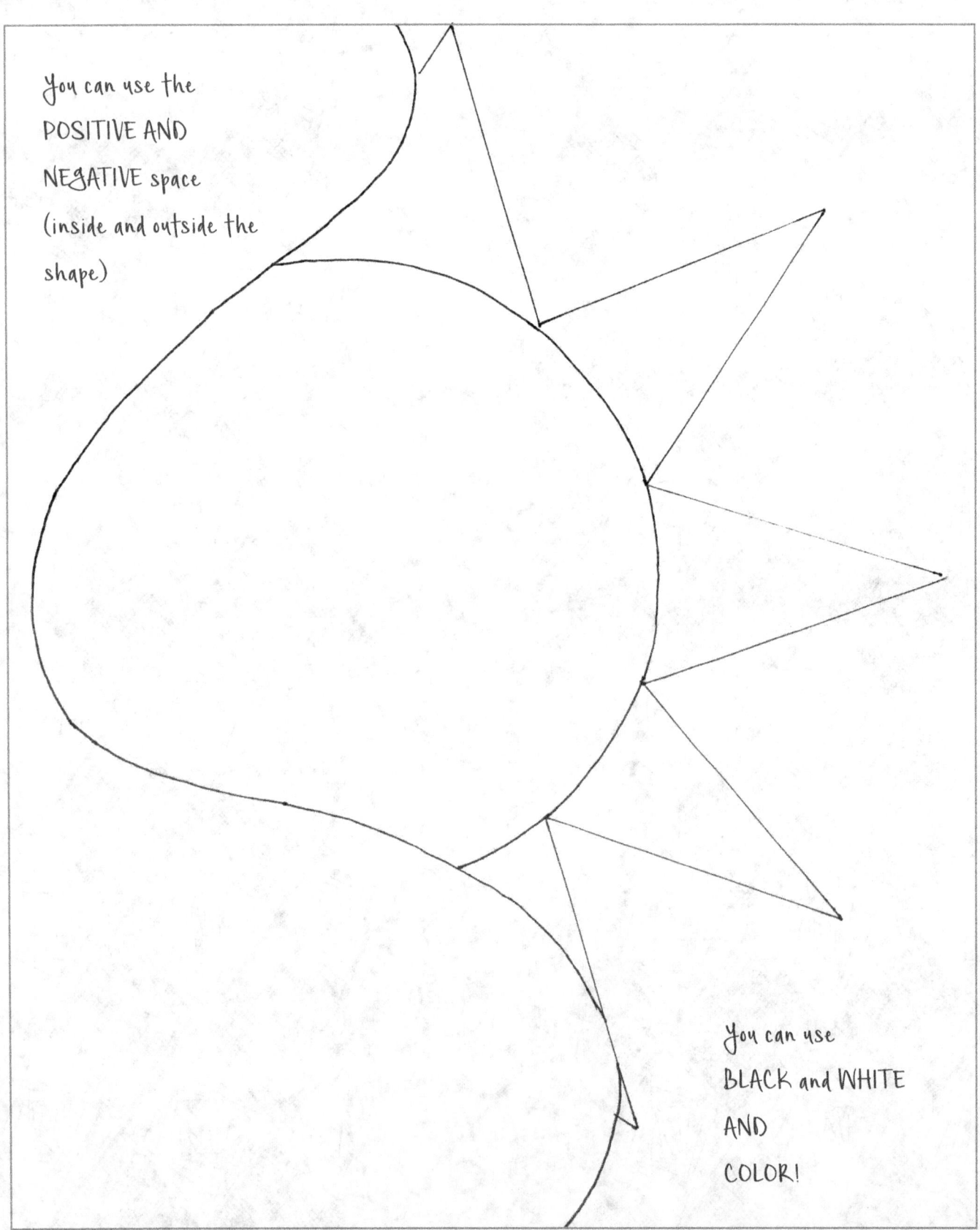

You can use the
POSITIVE AND
NEGATIVE space
(inside and outside the
shape)

You can use
BLACK and WHITE
AND
COLOR!

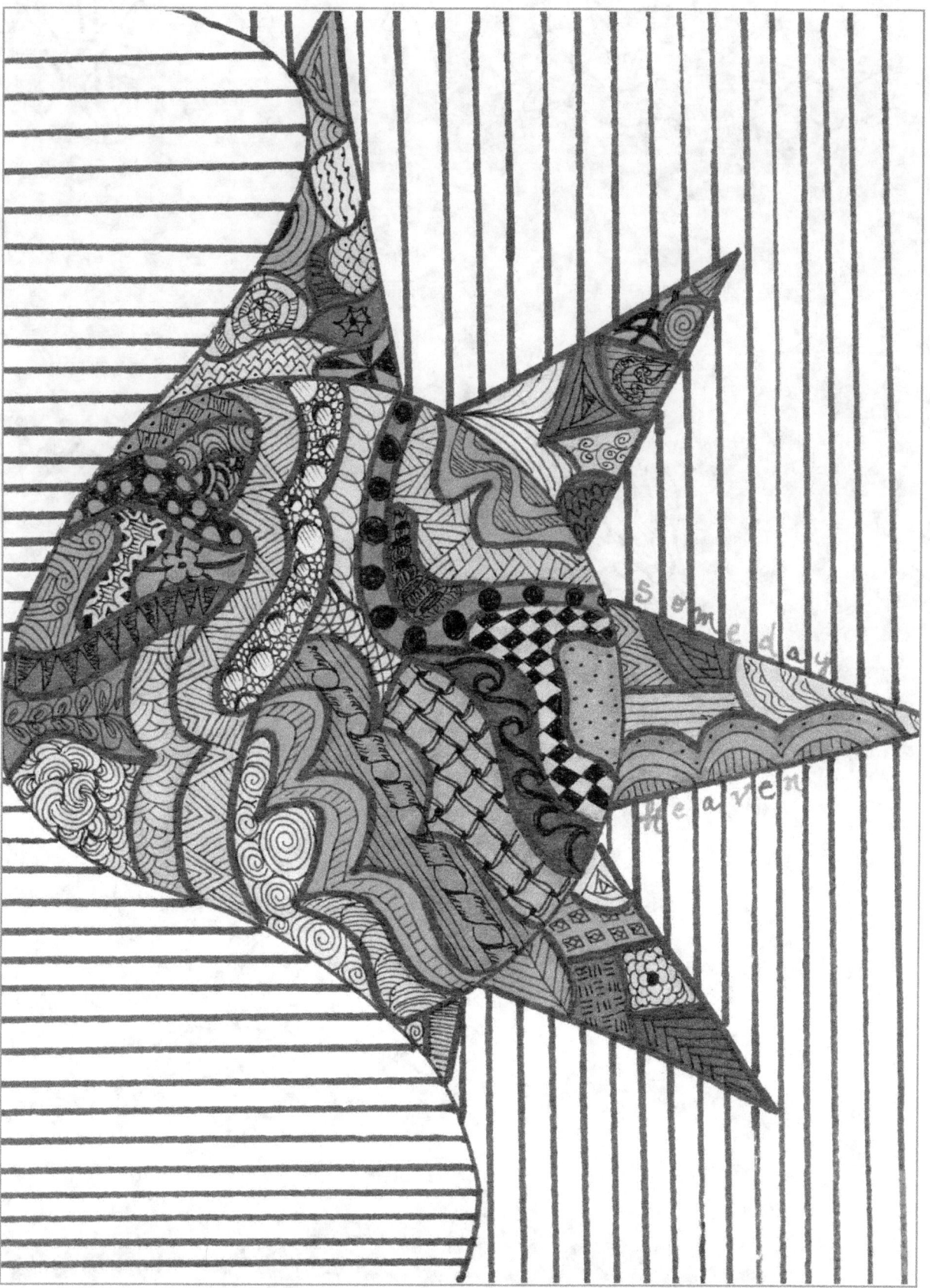

Lily and Emma, always remember the fingernail moon.

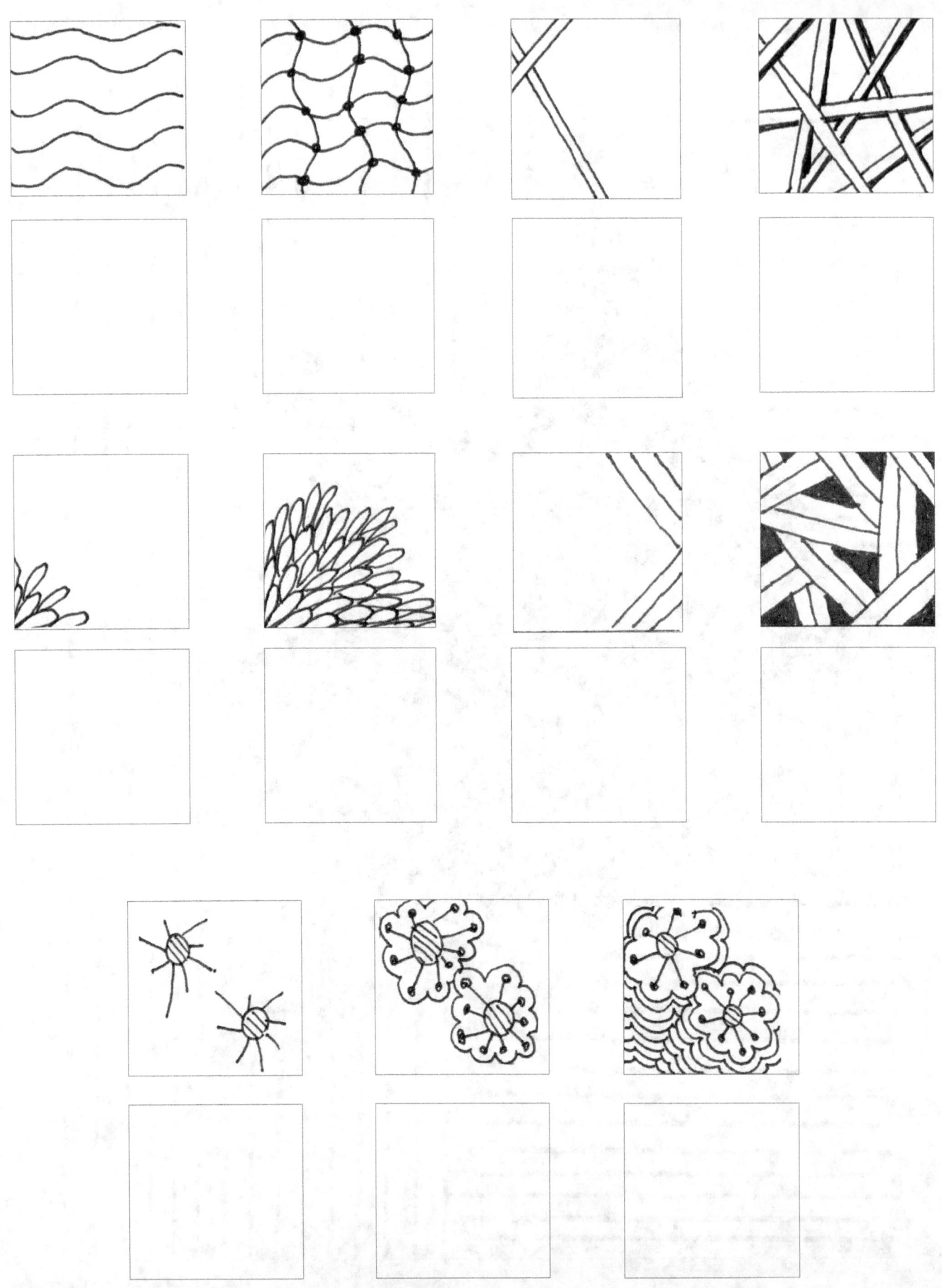

Doodle Me This

Doodle me this...

Are you improving? Yeay You!

Do you love the markers, pens and tools you are using?

If not change them!

If so, use them!

Are you allowing yourself to fail? AWESOME!

Remember miskates help you grow. Are you growing?

Teach a few doodles to friends. They will be impressed!

I had a few friends over for tea and taught them the

elephant doodle. I brought the template on a postcard.

(Cardstock cut in half)

 They left with a card and a bit of confidence.

Over time your self-confidence as an artist,

whether novice or pro, will increase.

YES, I said artist!

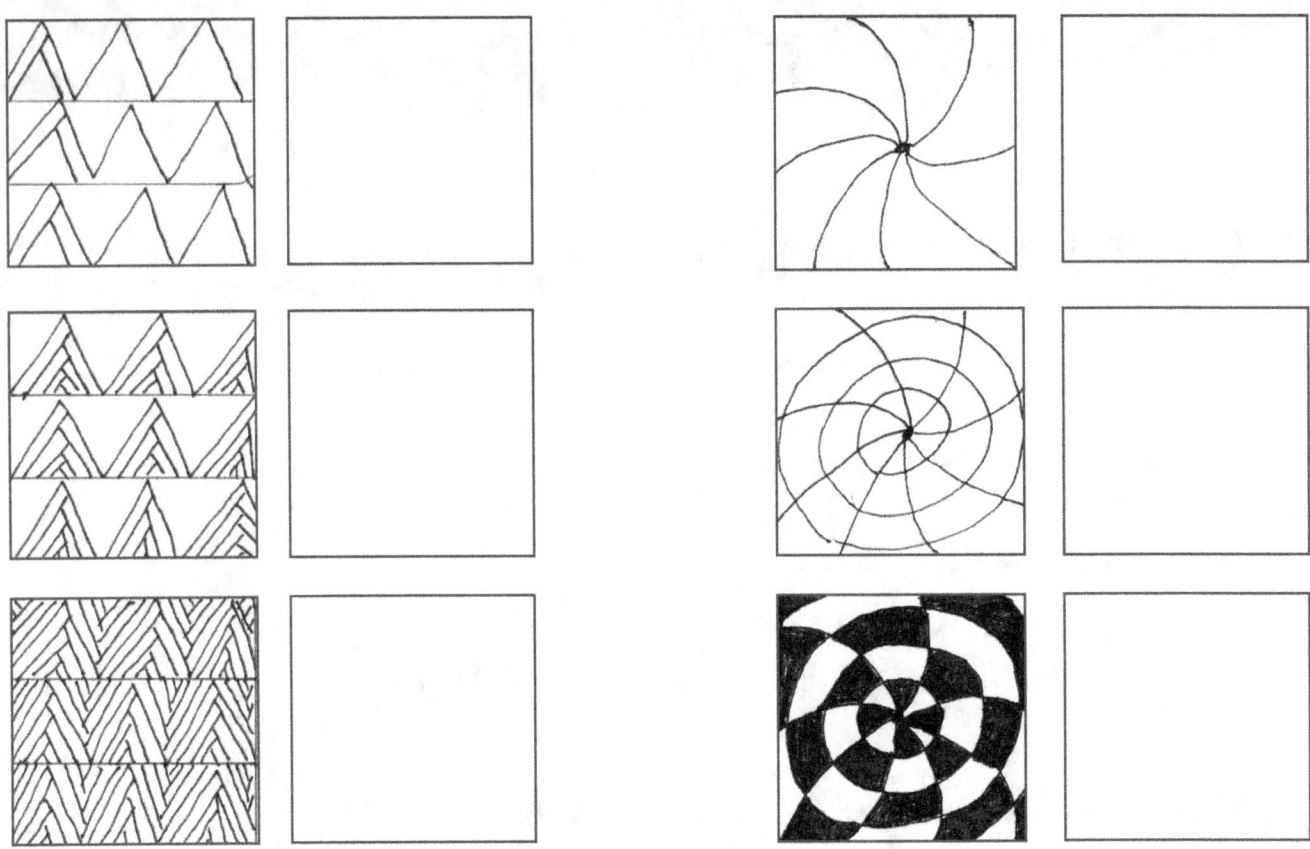

get creative!

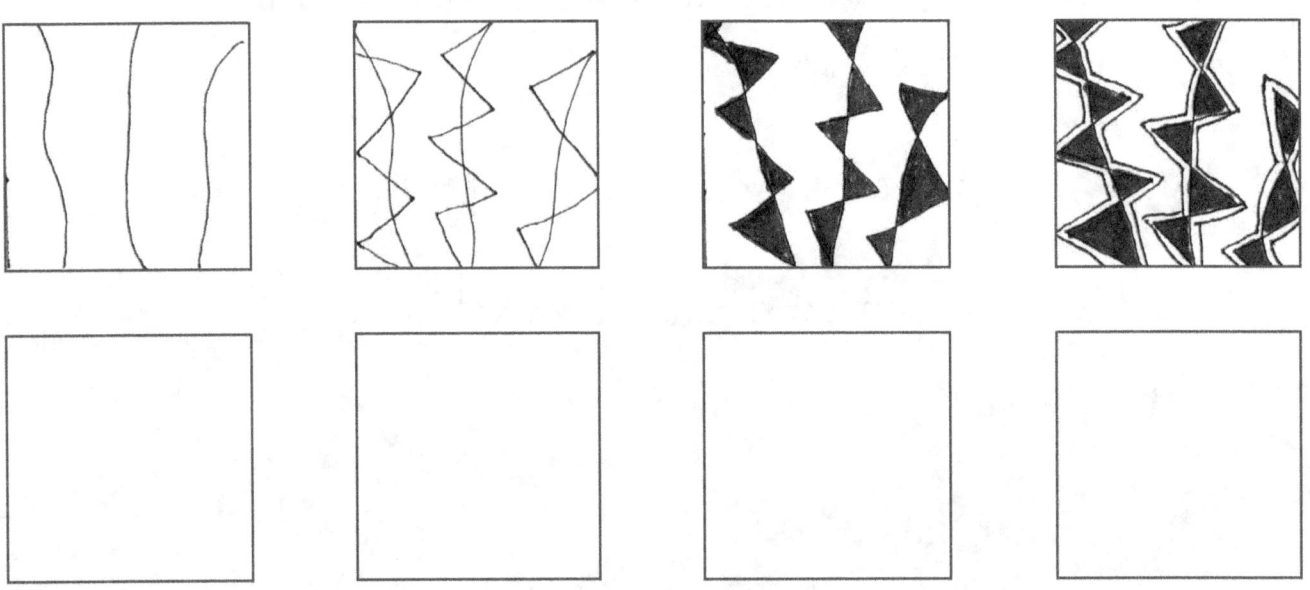

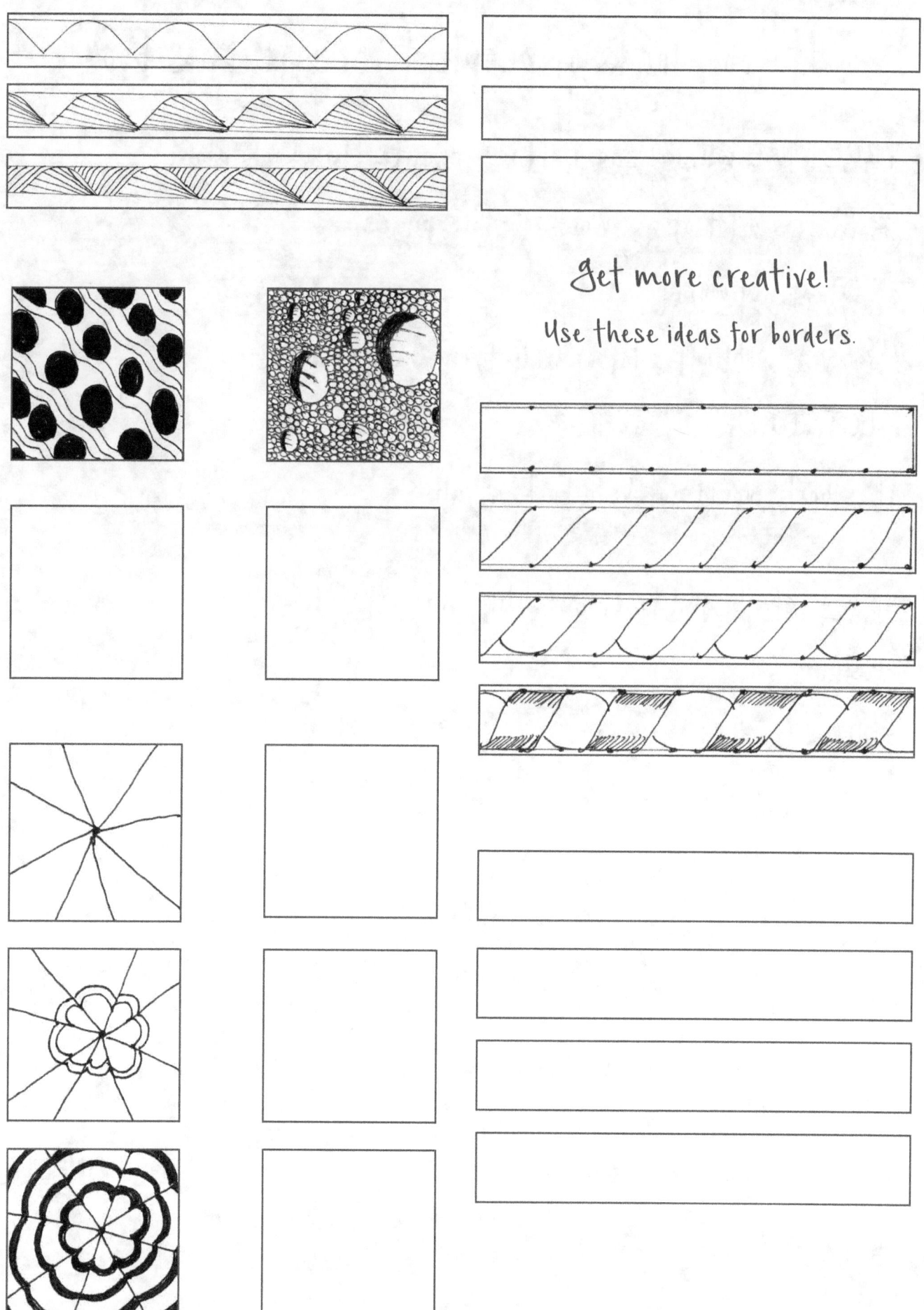

get more creative!

Use these ideas for borders.

It took loads of people to create this book.

TRUST ME when I say, I did not create this book alone!

Yeah, it's a lot of my work on the pages,

a LOT of my work.

However, without a lot of help from my friends,

a LOT of help,

this book would not be a book at all...

To my family and friends (online and off) who:

~helped

~edited (and edited again!)

~encouraged

and

~PRAYED.

Thank you.

Thank you from the bottom of my heart.